Language to go

INTERMEDIATE

STUDENTS' BOOK

Araminta Crace
Robin Wileman

Series Editor: Simon Greenall

Longman

v.longman.com

www.language-to-go.com

The past

Lesson 1 It's absolutely true! PAGE 4
Language to go: Telling stories and exaggerating events
Vocabulary and speaking: Adjectives and intensifiers
Listening: Rio Carnival
Grammar: Past simple and continuous
Get talking and writing: Telling a true story

The present

Lesson 2 Are you a morning person? PAGE 6
Language to go: Asking about and describing routines
Vocabulary and speaking: Sleep
Reading: Extract from *Nice Work*
Grammar: Subject and object questions
Get talking: A class survey

The future

Lesson 3 What's in a name? PAGE 8
Language to go: Making decisions and giving reasons for decisions
Vocabulary and speaking: Associations
Listening: Reasons for naming a baby
Grammar: Future with *will* and *going to*
Get talking: Choosing names for products

Vocabulary

Lesson 4 Career paths PAGE 10
Language to go: Comparing careers
Vocabulary and speaking: Education
Reading: *Studying? Is it really worth it?*
Grammar: Comparatives and superlatives
Get talking: Comparing lives and careers

Modals

Lesson 5 On the other hand PAGE 12
Language to go: Describing abilities and difficulties
Vocabulary and speaking: Levels of difficulty
Listening: Being left-handed
Grammar: Modal verbs for ability
Get talking: An ability test

Connecting

Lesson 6 Corporate spying PAGE 14
Language to go: Describing reasons for actions
Vocabulary and speaking: Crime
Reading: *Someone's watching you!*
Grammar: Adverbs of purpose
Get talking and writing: roleplay: A meeting about company security

The perfect

Lesson 7 Teamwork PAGE 16
Language to go: Talking about your experience
Vocabulary and speaking: Work
Listening: A job interview
Grammar: Present perfect simple
Get talking: roleplay: A job interview

Functions

Lesson 8 Nice to meet you PAGE 18
Language to go: What to say in social situations
Vocabulary and speaking: Topics of conversation
Listening: A chance meeting
Function: Managing a conversation
Get talking and writing: Small talk

Conditionals

Lesson 9 Australia PAGE 20
Language to go: Making suggestions to visitors to your area
Vocabulary and speaking: Travel items
Reading: *The Australian Outback*
Grammar: First conditional
Get talking and writing: Advising visitors to your area

Verb patterns

Lesson 10 Take it easy PAGE 22
Language to go: Discussing sport
Vocabulary: Expressions with *take*
Listening and speaking: An evening in?
Grammar: Verb constructions for likes and dislikes
Get talking: Comparing opinions about sport

Lesson 11 Determination PAGE 24
Language to go: Comparing past and present habits
Vocabulary and speaking: Determination
Listening: Modern-day addicts
Grammar: *Used to* and *would*
Get talking: Things you did as a child

Lesson 12 Money matters PAGE 26
Language to go: Talking about money
Vocabulary and speaking: Money and banks
Reading: *e-banking*
Grammar: Verbs with two objects
Get talking: Dividing up your winnings

Lesson 13 The river PAGE 28
Language to go: Describing plans for a trip
Vocabulary and speaking: Phrasal verbs about tourism
Listening: A trip on the Thames
Grammar: Present simple and continuous for future
Get talking: Planning a day trip

Lesson 14 Radio wedding PAGE 30
Language to go: Talking about relationships
Vocabulary and speaking: Weddings
Reading: *Two strangers and a wedding*
Vocabulary 2: Uses of *get*
Get talking and writing: What makes a good marriage?

Lesson 15 Less is more PAGE 32
Language to go: Giving advice
Vocabulary and speaking: *Waste, use, spend, save* + noun
Listening: Managing your life
Grammar: Modal verbs for giving advice
Get talking and writing: Solving problems

Lesson 16 Looks good! PAGE 34
Language to go: Defining people, things, time and place
Vocabulary and speaking: The five senses
Reading: *Smells that work*
Grammar: Defining relative clauses
Get talking: Favourite sights and sounds

Lesson 17 Changes PAGE 36
Language to go: Describing recent changes
Vocabulary and speaking: Lifestyle: word building
Reading and listening: Feng Shui
Grammar: Present perfect simple with *yet, already, just*
Get talking: Discussing changes in your life

Lesson 18 How polite are you? PAGE 38
Language to go: Making and responding to requests
Vocabulary and speaking: Phrasal verbs: *turn, switch, go*
Reading: Quiz: *Excuse me ...*
Function: Informal and polite requests
Get talking: Asking people to do things

Lesson 19 Going alone PAGE 40
Language to go: Talking about hypothetical situations
Vocabulary and speaking: Adjectives describing loneliness and fear
Reading: *100 days at sea*
Grammar: Second conditional
Get talking: How would you feel if ... ?

Lesson 20 What's in the fridge? PAGE 42
Language to go: Talking about food and cooking
Vocabulary and speaking: Food and cooking
Listening: Two chefs
Grammar: Verb constructions with *-ing* / infinitive
Get talking: Discussing cooking and eating habits

> Information for pair and group work PAGE 84   > Practice section PAGE 88   > Grammar reference PAGE 108

Lesson 21 Airport PAGE 44

Language to go: Recounting events in your life
Vocabulary and speaking: Travel and airports
Reading: Newspaper extract: *The Hub*
Grammar: Past perfect simple
Get talking and writing: Sharing stories

Lesson 22 A star is born ... or made? PAGE 46

Language to go: Describing a process
Vocabulary and speaking: Fame and success
Listening: Creation of a pop legend
Grammar: Passive constructions
Get talking: Information gap: The Williams sisters

Lesson 23 The future of toys PAGE 48

Language to go: Making predictions about the future
Vocabulary and speaking: Toys and games
Reading: *Tomorrow's toys*
Grammar: Modal verbs to talk about future probability
Get talking and writing: Future products

Lesson 24 I'll call you PAGE 50

Language to go: Communicating by phone
Speaking and vocabulary: Telephoning expressions
Listening: A telephone conversation
Vocabulary 2: Phrasal verbs about telephoning
Get talking: roleplay: On the phone

Lesson 25 Do the right thing PAGE 52

Language to go: Describing rules in the present
Vocabulary and speaking: *Make* and *do*
Reading: *Netiquette*
Grammar: Modal verbs for necessity and obligation
Get talking and writing: Discussing 'rules' of behaviour

Lesson 26 Six and a half hours PAGE 54

Language to go: Comparing attitudes
Vocabulary and speaking: Expressions with *time*
Reading: *Long-distance commuter*
Grammar: Ways to express contrasting ideas
Get talking and writing: Attitudes to work and time

Lesson 27 Achievement PAGE 56

Language to go: Discussing personal achievements and projects
Vocabulary and speaking: Achievements and projects
Listening: Trevor Baylis – inventor
Grammar: Present perfect simple and continuous
Get talking and writing: What you've been doing

Lesson 28 Long walk to freedom PAGE 58

Language to go: Discussing freedom
Vocabulary and speaking: Prison
Reading: Extracts from *Long Walk to Freedom*
Function: Prohibition, obligation and permission in the past
Get talking: Comparing freedom at different times of your life

Lesson 29 Shaking hands PAGE 60

Language to go: Talking about likely and unlikely situations
Speaking and vocabulary: Doing business
Reading and listening: Business around the world
Grammar: First and second conditionals
Get talking: Discussing reactions to situations

Lesson 30 Sunshine and showers PAGE 62

Language to go: Reporting what you hear or read
Vocabulary and speaking: The weather
Listening: Ways of forecasting the weather
Grammar: Reported statements
Get talking: Reporting the weather

Lesson 31 Turning points PAGE 64

Language to go: Talking about important moments
Vocabulary and speaking: Things we read
Reading: *A suitcase of stories*
Grammar: Past perfect simple and continuous
Get talking: Turning points in your life

Lesson 32 Clean and tidy PAGE 66

Language to go: Talking about things people do for you
Vocabulary and speaking: Housework and cleanliness
Reading: *Maid4U – Services for your home*
Grammar: *Have something done* and reflexive pronouns
Get talking: Things you do, and have done for you

Lesson 33 Tomorrow's world PAGE 68

Language to go: Predicting future events
Vocabulary and speaking: Describing changes
Listening: Future inventions
Grammar: Future with *will* and *will have done*
Get talking: What will you have done by 2020?

Lesson 34 Honeymoon horrors PAGE 70

Language to go: Describing symptoms of an illness
Vocabulary and speaking: Medical problems and symptoms
Listening: Honeymoon horror stories
Vocabulary 2: Phrasal verbs about illness
Get talking: roleplay: A visit to the doctor

Lesson 35 Ice maiden PAGE 72

Language to go: Drawing conclusions about the past
Vocabulary: People and groups
Speaking and reading: *An amazing discovery*
Grammar: Past modal verbs of deduction
Get talking and writing: Life 2,500 years ago

Lesson 36 A winning formula PAGE 74

Language to go: Giving extra information
Vocabulary and speaking: Business processes: word building
Reading: *A simple idea*
Grammar: Non-defining relative clauses
Get talking and writing: Explaining a business plan

Lesson 37 Old friends PAGE 76

Language to go: Describing friendship
Vocabulary and speaking: Verb expressions about friendship
Listening: Old friends
Grammar: Present perfect with *for* and *since*
Get talking: Telling someone about a good friend

Lesson 38 Don't worry, be happy PAGE 78

Language to go: Asking questions about personal issues
Speaking and vocabulary: Happiness
Listening: Survey about happiness
Function: Polite questions
Get talking: Personal issues

Lesson 39 If only ... PAGE 80

Language to go: Talking about past regrets
Vocabulary and speaking: Shopping
Reading: Extract from *Are You Experienced?*
Grammar: Third conditional and *I wish / If only*
Get talking: You only regret what you don't do

Lesson 40 How did it go? PAGE 82

Language to go: Reporting a conversation or interview
Speaking and vocabulary: Job applications and interviews
Listening: After the interview
Grammar: Reported questions
Get talking: Reporting a conversation

The past

The present

The future

Vocabulary

Modals

Connecting

The perfect

Functions

Conditionals

Verb patterns

Vocabulary   Adjectives and intensifiers
Grammar   Past simple and continuous
Language to go   Telling stories and exaggerating events

It's absolutely true!

Vocabulary and speaking

1   Look at the photos of Carnival in Rio de Janeiro, Brazil. In pairs, discuss the following questions.

   1   Have you been to Rio for Carnival?
   2   Would you like to go? Why? / Why not?
   3   What do you know about it?

2   Match the pairs of adjectives which are similar in meaning.

   Example: hot – boiling (= very, very hot)

   > hot fascinating good packed boiling interesting
   > tired enormous crowded bad big fantastic
   > awful exhausted

3   Describe the photos using the adjectives from Exercise 2.

4   Complete the dialogues below with a suitable adjective or intensifier.

   1   A: Were you _____ hot?
      B: Hot? I was absolutely _____ !
   2   A: Were you really _____ ?
      B: Yes, I was _____ exhausted!
   3   A: Was it _____ crowded?
      B: Yes, it was really _____ !
   4   A: Was the stadium _____ big?
      B: Big? It was absolutely _____ !
   5   A: Was the music _____ ?
      B: Good? It was _____ fantastic!

   Now listen and check your answers. When do we use the intensifiers *really*, *very* and *absolutely*?

Listening

5  Listen to Sara talking about her visit to Carnival. What did she think of it?

6 Listen again. Are these sentences true (T) or false (F)?

1 Sara was staying in Rio.
2 It was raining when she arrived.
3 They were planning to cancel the carnival because of the rain.
4 When the rain stopped, the carnival started.
5 An audience of 70,000 was waiting in the Sambadrome.

7 Look again at the sentences above. <u>Underline</u> verbs in the past simple and ⊙circle⊙ verbs in the past continuous.

Grammar focus

8 Combine these sentences to make rules about the past simple and the past continuous.

1 The past simple ...
2 The past continuous ...
3 Sometimes the past continuous ...

a) ... is used to describe a longer action or event which is interrupted by an action or event in the past simple tense.

b) ... describes an action or event in the past.

c) ... describes a situation over a period of time in the past. It is often used to set the context to a story.

Practice

9 Complete the sentences using the correct form of the verbs in brackets.

Example: I *met* (meet) Tom yesterday while I *was waiting* (wait) for a bus.

1 I _____ (go) to the cinema twice last weekend.
2 He _____ (drive) very fast, when he _____ (see) a dog run across the road in front of him.
3 Julia _____ (listen) to loud music, so she _____ (not / hear) the doorbell.
4 _____ (you / see) Pablo at the party? He _____ (wear) an orange shirt.
5 I _____ (make) a lovely dinner, but he wasn't hungry so he _____ (not / eat) anything.
6 I _____ (enjoy) the lesson so much yesterday that I _____ (not / realise) it was time to go.

Get talking ...

10 In pairs, tell your partner a true story about you.

First set the context. Then describe the action but exaggerate some of the information to make the story more interesting. These ideas may help you.

- You met a famous person
- You did something very dangerous
- You had an accident
- You went to a strange place
- You found something interesting
- You fell in love

Your partner must decide which information is true and which information is exaggerated.

... and writing

11 Write your story as part of an informal letter to a friend. Exaggerate some of the story to make it more interesting.

Language to go

A: I saw her when I was walking down the road.
B: Did she look good?
A: Good? She looked absolutely fantastic!

> GRAMMAR REFERENCE PAGE 108
> PRACTICE PAGE 88

LESSON 2
The present

Vocabulary   Sleep
Grammar   Subject and object questions
Language to go   Asking about and describing routines

Are you a morning person?

A

B

C

Vocabulary and speaking

1   **In pairs, discuss the following questions.**

What is your favourite / least favourite part of the day? Why?

2   **Match the phrases about sleep with the correct definitions.**

Phrases	Definitions
1 a morning person	a) sleep longer than planned
2 stay up late	b) a person who feels good / alert in the mornings
3 oversleep	c) a person who gets up early
4 have an early night	d) stop sleeping
5 not be able to keep (your) eyes open	e) begin to sleep
6 have a lie-in	f) go to bed later than usual
7 be an early riser	g) stay in bed later than usual
8 wake up	h) go to bed earlier than usual
9 fall asleep	i) be in a bad mood in the morning
10 get out of bed on the wrong side	j) find it difficult to stay awake at times during the day

3   **Describe the people in the pictures using the phrases from Exercise 2.**

Reading

4   **Read the text and say which of the pictures are described.**

Vic has eaten his two slices of toast and is on his third cup of tea and first cigarette of the day when Marjorie enters the kitchen in her dressing gown and slippers.

'Smoking,' she says, condensing into a single word an argument well known to both of them. Vic grunts. He glances at the kitchen clock.

'Shouldn't Sandra and Gary be getting up? I won't waste my breath on Raymond.'

'Gary doesn't have school today. The teachers are on strike.'

'What about Sandra?'

'I'm taking her to the doctor's.'

'What's the matter with her?'

Marjorie yawns evasively. 'Oh, nothing serious.'

'Why can't she go on her own? A girl of seventeen should be able to go to the doctor's without someone to hold her hand.'

'I don't go in with her, not unless she wants me to. I just wait with her.'

Vic regards his wife suspiciously. 'You're not going shopping with her afterwards?'

Marjorie blushes. 'Well, she needs a new pair of shoes ...'

Adapted from *Nice Work* by David Lodge

5 Read the text again and answer the questions.

1 What did Vic have for breakfast?
2 What does Marjorie think about smoking?
3 Who got out of bed on the wrong side?
4 Who should be getting up?
5 Which child often oversleeps?
6 What do Vic and Marjorie talk about?

Grammar focus

6 Look at the examples and <u>underline</u> the correct alternatives in sentences 1–4.

> A Subject questions: *Who speaks* to Vic?
>   Answer: Marjorie speaks to Vic.
>
> B Object questions: *Who does* Vic *speak* to?
>   Answer: He speaks to Marjorie.

1 In A, Marjorie is *the subject / the object.*
2 In B, Marjorie is *the subject / the object.*
3 *Subject questions / Object questions* need an auxiliary verb.
4 When we ask questions about the subject of the sentence, the word order of the question and the answer is *the same / different.*

7 Look at Exercise 5 again and answer the questions.

1 Which *auxiliary verbs* are used?
2 Which are *subject questions* and which are *object questions*?

Practice

8 Look at the prompts and write the questions. Use the answers to help you decide if it is a subject or object question.

Example: got up / first? *Who got up first?* Vic.

1 Marjorie / wear?	Dressing gown and slippers.
2 Vic / speak to / first?	Marjorie.
3 like / have a lie-in?	All the children.
4 Vic / glance at?	The kitchen clock.
5 take / Sandra to the doctor's?	Her mother is.
6 Marjorie / plan to do after the doctor's?	Go shopping.
7 Marjorie / say about the teachers?	They are on strike.

Get talking

9 Do a survey to find the morning people in your class.

1 Complete the questions using the prompts.

2 Do the questionnaire in pairs, then discuss your answers in groups.

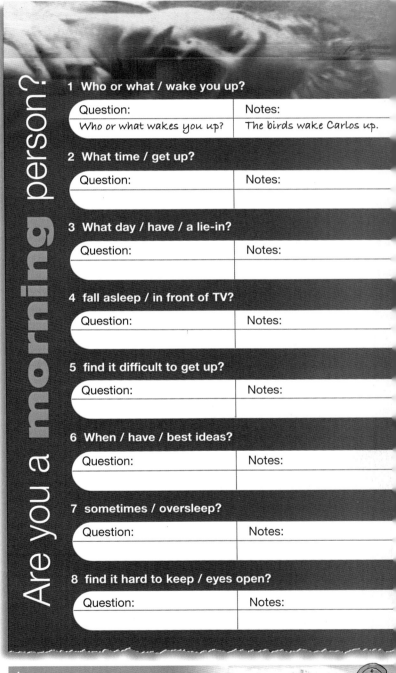

Are you a morning person?

1 Who or what / wake you up?

Question:	Notes:
Who or what wakes you up?	The birds wake Carlos up.

2 What time / get up?

Question:	Notes:

3 What day / have / a lie-in?

Question:	Notes:

4 fall asleep / in front of TV?

Question:	Notes:

5 find it difficult to get up?

Question:	Notes:

6 When / have / best ideas?

Question:	Notes:

7 sometimes / oversleep?

Question:	Notes:

8 find it hard to keep / eyes open?

Question:	Notes:

Language to go

> A: What wakes you up in the morning?
> B: A large coffee!

> GRAMMAR REFERENCE PAGE 108
> PRACTICE PAGE 88

LESSON **3**
The future

Vocabulary Associations
Grammar Future with *will* and *going to*
Language to go Making decisions and giving reasons for decisions

What's in a name?

Vocabulary and speaking

1 Complete the sentences using the words in the box.

> go with   image   associations   makes   reminds
> sounds   suggests   suits

1 The name Elvis always _____ me of a rock star.
2 Her name's Flora. That _____ a flower to me.
3 She's called India, so it _____ me think of the country.
4 My name doesn't _____ my personality at all. It means 'calm' – and I'm not!
5 I think a name like Augustus creates a very strong _____ .
6 His first name's Jorge, so it _____ like he could be Spanish.
7 She's a lively person and her name means 'full of life', so it really _____ her.
8 The name Lorna has all kinds of happy _____ for me, because that was my grandmother's name.

2 In pairs, discuss the following questions.

1 Do you like your name?
2 Does it go with your personality?
3 Do you know why your parents gave you that name?
4 Do you know what it means?

Listening

3 Look at the pictures. They show ways in which parents decide on names for their children. Think of other ideas.

4 🔊 Listen to parents talking about their children's names. As you listen, write the speaker next to the name(s) they chose.

Name	Speaker	Reason
Dawn		
Lola		
Kevin		
George		
Stanley	Speaker 1	
Matilda		

5 Look at the Top Ten reasons why parents choose names for their children. Listen again and match the six names in Exercise 4 with the correct reasons.

> **Top 10 reasons for naming baby...**
>
> 1 It sounds good.
> 2 It's a famous person's name.
> 3 It came from a name book.
> 4 It's a traditional family name.
> 5 It creates a strong image.
> 6 It reminds them of a close friend.
> 7 It suits the baby's appearance.
> 8 It's the name of a parent or grandparent.
> 9 It has religious associations.
> 10 It refers to the time of birth.

Grammar focus

6 **Match the examples in the box with the rules below.**

> A We*'ll take* the first name we find.
> B We*'re going to call* our baby boy Stanley.
> C I *don't think* I*'ll call* her that.

1 When we talk about decisions made *before* the moment of speaking. Example ___
2 When we talk about decisions made *at* the moment of speaking. Example ___
3 When we make a decision *not* to do something. Example ___

7 🎧 **Listen and repeat the sentences.**

Practice

8 **Underline the correct form of the verb.**

Example: We've already made our decision; *he'll* / *he's going to* be called Bernie.

1 We decided last night that *we'll* / *we're going to* have a party to celebrate Dave's new job.
2 A: Do you want to come to the new Bond movie tonight?
   B: I'm not sure. *I'll* / *I'm going to* call you later.
3 What did you decide – *will you* / *are you going to* call your dog Bones?
4 A: Oh, no! Did you hear that? The train*'s going to* / *will* be half an hour late.
   B: In that case *I'll* / *I'm going to* take the bus.
5 I haven't made up my mind yet, but I think *I'll* / *I'm going to* call my boat *Gypsy Queen*.
6 A: Would you like a drink?
   B: No, I don't think *I will* / *I'm going to*, thanks. I had one earlier.
7 I've made up my mind – the twins *won't* / *aren't going to* have similar names.

Get talking

9 **Look at the products below and think about the best names for each one.**

1 Klok / Time-zone / Accurate
2 Go Go Go / Like You / Undercover
3 Sparkle / White Magic / Fresh
4 Rainbow / Tasty / Tropical
5 Yum Yum! / Five-star Hotel / Simply Delicious

1 First decide which name you like best and why. Choose one of the names suggested (or think of other ideas).
2 In groups, try to agree on the best names. Remember to give your reasons.

Language to go

A: Are you going to marry him then?
B: I'm not sure, Dad. I'll decide later.

> GRAMMAR REFERENCE PAGE 108
> PRACTICE PAGE 89

LESSON 4
Vocabulary

Vocabulary   Education
Grammar   Comparatives and superlatives
Language to go   Comparing careers

Career paths

Vocabulary and speaking

1   **Match the nouns and verbs to complete the spidergrams.**

> school   a job   a test   a degree
> an exam   qualifications   college
> university   good grades

qualifications

get

go to / leave

take / pass / fail

2   **In pairs, discuss the following questions.**

1   Do exam results really show your true ability?
2   How important are qualifications?

Reading

3   **Read the article quickly to find out what jobs Gavin and Carl do now.**

4   **Read the article again. Are the statements true (T) or false (F)?**

1   Young people will get their exam results today.
2   Gavin always wanted to teach history.
3   Gavin lost his job because he was the oldest lecturer.
4   Gavin thinks re-training is easier for young people than it is for him.
5   Carl did well at school.
6   Carl gave up the training course because it was difficult.
7   Carl is successful because he has worked hard.
8   Carl thinks exams are necessary.

Studying? Is it really worth it?

It's that time of year again – the national exam results are coming out today and young people all over the country are deciding what to do next. Go to college? Get a job? So, it's a good time to ask: 'How important is education if you want to be successful in life?'

A job for life?

A university education used to be the safest path – a job for life. Is this still true? Read Gavin's story.

'I always loved history but I didn't know what job I wanted. I worked hard at school, passed all my exams and went to university to study history. After continuing studying and becoming a university lecturer, I thought I had a good job and a safe career. Unfortunately, the university reduced the teaching staff. I was the most experienced lecturer, but also the most expensive so I had to leave. I'm 51 now. I want to re-train but it's harder for me than it is for younger people.'

Grammar focus

5 **Look at the examples and answer the questions.**

> A Re-training is *harder* for me *than* it is for younger people.
> B Studying is *more important than* working.
> C He was *the oldest* lecturer.
> D It was *the most boring* thing I ever did.
> E I was *the most experienced* lecturer.

1 What are the rules for making comparative and superlative sentences?
2 How do you pronounce *than* in comparative sentences?
3 How do you pronounce *the* and *most* (e.g. *the most successful*) in superlative sentences?

6 Listen to the sentences and repeat them with the correct pronunciation.

A lesson in life?

Carl's chosen route would appear to be the riskiest, but could it actually be the most successful in the modern world?

'I was the worst pupil in my school and left at 16. I tried a training course, but it was the most boring thing I ever did and I gave up after a week! I got a job in an electrical shop, and quickly learnt enough to become manager. Through hard work, I made my way to the top and now I'm Managing Director of one of the biggest software companies in Europe. Who needs exams? Work is a much better way to learn than any courses!'

Practice

7 **Rewrite the sentences so that they have the same meaning.**

Example: Gavin was a more successful student than Carl. Carl was <u>a less successful</u> <u>student than Gavin</u>.

1 Carl had a worse education than Gavin.
  Gavin had _____ .
2 Cambridge University is older than Yale University.
  Yale University _____ .
3 Carl's career path was riskier than Gavin's.
  Gavin's career path _____ .
4 Gavin wasn't the cheapest lecturer.
  Gavin was _____ .
5 Carl wasn't the most interested student in his school.
  Carl was _____ .
6 Today's test was harder than last week's test.
  Last week's test _____ .

Get talking

8 **In groups, look at the information about three different people on page 84. Compare them using the suggestions in the box.**

> happy   satisfied   friends
> tired   stressed   rich
> free time   benefits

Example: I think James is the richest, but he probably has the least free time.

Language to go

> A: What's the best thing about your new job?
> B: Well, I've got a bigger desk and longer holidays!

> GRAMMAR REFERENCE PAGE 108
> PRACTICE PAGE 89

Vocabulary   Levels of difficulty
Grammar   Modal verbs for ability
Language to go   Describing abilities and difficulties

On the other hand

Vocabulary and speaking

1   Put the expressions into the correct column below.

It was …
I found it …

| a piece of cake. |
| hard. |
| manageable. |
| impossible. |
| complicated. |
| no trouble. |
| simple. |
| straightforward. |
| tough. |
| possible. |

Easy	OK	Difficult
a piece of cake	*manageable*	*hard*

 Now listen and repeat the expressions with the correct pronunciation.

2   Look at the photos of people learning to do things. In pairs, discuss the following questions.

How did you feel when you first …

• spoke English?
• used the Internet?
• rode a bicycle?
• learned to tie your shoelaces?

3   How much do you know about being left-handed? In pairs, discuss the following questions. Then check the answers on page 84.

1   What does being 'left-handed' mean?
2   What does being 'ambidextrous' mean?
3   What percentage of people are left-handed?
4   Do we inherit left-handedness and right-handedness?

Listening

4    Listen to the first part of the conversation between Mike and Joanna talking about being left-handed. Tick (✓) the things they mention.

1   tennis ☐
2   driving ☐
3   writing ☐
4   eating ☐
5   drawing ☐
6   being ambidextrous ☐

(A) (B) (C) (D)

5 🔊 The pictures above show four ability tests that Mike and Joanna did with their right hands. Listen to the rest of their conversation and write notes about how they got on.

	Mike	Joanna
1 Throw a ball		
2 Write a message		
3 Cut with scissors		
4 Draw a face		

Grammar focus

6 Look at the recording script on page 118 and find examples of talking about ability and difficulty.

Example: *I managed to throw the ball OK.*

7 Complete the rules using the correct form of *can, could, be able to* or *manage to.*

1 When we talk about ability in the present, we use _____ .

2 When we talk about permanent ability in the past, we use _____ .

3 When we talk about something that was possible on a specific occasion, we use _____ or _____ (but not *could*).

4 When we talk about something that was NOT possible on a specific occasion, we use _____ or _____ or _____ .

Practice

8 Complete the sentences using the correct form of *can, could, be able to* or *manage to*. There may be more than one answer.

Example: The homework was difficult but in the end I **managed** to do it.

1 I _____ write until I was eight.

2 This grammar's too complicated, I _____ understand it.

3 Last year I _____ speak English much better than I _____ write it.

4 It's embarrassing, but I'm 29 and I still _____ ride a bike!

5 Even before he was seven, he _____ kick a football brilliantly with either foot.

6 I'm just _____ to cook. I burn everything!

7 My sister fell into a river but fortunately she _____ swim to the bank.

8 Could you repeat that, please? I _____ hear what you said.

Get talking

9 Do the ability tests that Mike and Joanna did.

1 In pairs, discuss how well you think you can do the tests with your 'other' hand.

2 Do the tests, then complete the table.

3 In groups, discuss your results.

	You	Partner
1 Throw a ball into a waste bin		
2 Write a message		
3 Cut paper with scissors		
4 Draw a face		

Language to go

A: Did you manage to fix the car?

B: Yes, it was a piece of cake!

> GRAMMAR REFERENCE PAGE 109
> PRACTICE PAGE 90

LESSON **6**
Connecting

Vocabulary Crime
Grammar Adverbs of purpose
Language to go Describing reasons for actions

Corporate spying

Vocabulary and speaking

1 **Look at the sentences and <u>underline</u> the correct alternatives.**

1 The security guard spent the night *looking at* / *spying on* the CCTV monitors.
2 *Muggers* / *Thieves* broke into the bank last night and *borrowed* / *stole* £1 million.
3 Police didn't have enough *sentence* / *evidence* to arrest the *suspect* / *prisoner*.
4 The director was *accused* / *committed* of using company profits to buy jewellery for his wife.
5 George told me he was thirty, when really he's forty-five! He's so *dishonest* / *illegal*.
6 If you really didn't take the money, you must *deny* / *admit* it straightaway.

2 **Explain the difference in meaning between the pairs of words in *italics* in Exercise 1.**

3 **Do you think it is acceptable for employees to do these things at work?**

- take pens home
- send personal e-mails
- make personal phone calls
- claim too much on expense accounts

Reading

4 **Look at the photo in the newspaper article and describe what is happening.**

1 What are the security guards doing?
2 What are they looking for?

5 **Read the article quickly and match the headings below with the correct paragraphs.**

Ⓐ **They know where you are!**

Ⓑ **Do you take office pens?**

Ⓒ **Your computer can't hide.**

6 **Read the article again and answer the questions.**

1 What are video cameras and tape recorders used for at work?
2 Why do some companies put machines in their employees' cars?
3 What do you think 'virtual movements' in paragraph 3 means?

Someone'
watching you

Grammar focus

7 Complete the rules about the adverbs of purpose in the table by writing *verb*, *verb/-ing* or *subject + verb*. Find examples in the text to help you.

Ways of expressing purpose
Why someone does something …
1 *to +* <u>verb</u>   e.g. to watch employees' virtual movements
2 *in order to +* _____
3 *so as (not) to +* _____
4 *so that +* _____
Because something might happen …
5 *in case +* _____
What something is for …
6 *for +* _____

Admit it! Sometimes you make a few personal phone calls, you take home some office pens, you come back a bit late after lunch. You always thought nobody noticed. Nobody could accuse you of stealing! But not any more! From now on, employers will be taking advantage of new technology in order to spy on staff. And that means you!

You may not see them, but tiny tape recorders and video cameras are probably spying on you now. Security devices for watching and listening to everything that happens at the workplace. And don't try to hide! They can even check if workers are really where they say they are. Companies can link cameras to offices in case workers are tempted to steal property. They can install machines in sales representatives' cars so as to check on their expense accounts.

③

And what's more, businesses are bringing in IT security companies <u>to watch employees' virtual movements</u>. Software is installed so that they can record the websites you visit and check the e-mails you send. They find out all your secrets. You have been warned!

Practice

8 Write complete sentences using the prompts and a suitable connecting expression. There may be more than one answer.

Example: I'm getting a private detective / spy on my boyfriend
I'm getting a private detective to spy on my boyfriend.

1 He wants to buy one of those devices / recording phone conversations
2 She always carries a mobile phone / there's an emergency
3 Some companies use tapes and video cameras / find evidence of dishonest employees
4 Security cameras are used in shops / catch shoplifters
5 I've bought a new burglar alarm / anyone breaks into my house
6 They've got new window locks / nobody can open them from the outside

Get talking …

9 **In pairs, have a meeting about company security.**

Student A: You are the director of a company.
Turn to page 84 and read your information.

Student B: You are a sales representative from a security company.
Turn to page 86 and read your information.

… and writing

10 Write an e-mail to a colleague who could not attend the meeting. Summarise the main points of the meeting.

Language to go

A: Why are you putting in security cameras?
B: So that I know where I am.

> GRAMMAR REFERENCE PAGE 109
> PRACTICE PAGE 90

LESSON 7
The perfect

Vocabulary Work
Grammar Present perfect simple
Language to go Talking about your experience

Teamwork

Vocabulary and speaking

1 **In pairs, name the office equipment in the picture.**

Do you ever feel like this person?

2 **Match the verbs with the nouns to make expressions about things to do with work. There may be more than one answer.**

Verbs	Nouns
use	a job
send	a report
work in	an interview
organise	a promotion
apply for	an event
go for	a team
write	a fax
get	a computer
receive	an e-mail

In pairs, say which you have done.

Listening

3 **Look at the photo and the job advertisement. In pairs, discuss these questions.**

1 Do you think the applicant was successful?
2 Why? / Why not?

▨▨ **Now listen to the interview and check your ideas.**

4 **Listen again and make notes about what work experience Dan has and hasn't had.**

Team Leader required
to work in a busy team in a lively, young company.
Previous experience essential. Flexible hours. Use of car. Salary negotiable.
For an application form call
020 794 600 606

Applicant's name: Dan Gray

Interview time: 2.30 pm

Grammar focus

5 Look at the examples in the box and complete the sentences.

> A *Have* you ever *worked* in a team?
>   Yes, I *have*.
> B When did you do that?

1 The name of the tense in example A is: _____ .
2 The form of the tense is: _____ + _____ .
3 The name of the tense in example B is: _____ .

6 <u>Underline</u> the correct alternatives.

1 We use the *past simple / present perfect simple* to talk about our experiences. We *need / don't need* to say when the experiences happened.
2 We use the *past simple / present perfect simple* to talk about finished actions in the past. We *need / don't need* to say when it happened.

7 Look at the recording script on page 119 and find other examples of the present perfect simple.

Now listen and repeat the sentences.

Practice

8 Write dialogues with the correct form of the present perfect simple or past simple.

Example:

You / use / computer?	Yes
Have you ever used a computer?	*Yes, I have.*
When / learn?	In 2000
When did you learn?	*In 2000.*

1 You / organise / event?	No
2 You / work in / team?	Yes
When / do?	In March
3 You / send / fax?	No
4 You / apply for / job?	Yes
When / apply?	Last year
5 You / go for / promotion?	Yes
Be / successful?	Yes

9 In pairs, ask and answer the questions in Exercise 8, giving answers which are true for you.

Get talking

10 Roleplay an interview for the job advertised below.

1 In groups, prepare what you're going to say.
Group A are going to be interviewers.
Group B are going to be applicants.

> **Sales Manager – computers**
>
> **You have ...**
> • thought about a new job.
> • had international experience.
> • experienced past successes.
> • been a team leader.
> • run meetings in English.
>
> If you think you've done what it takes ... then we want to hear from you.

2 Do the interviews.

Language to go

A: Have you ever used English for business?
B: Yes, I have. I've given presentations in English.

> GRAMMAR REFERENCE PAGE 109
> PRACTICE PAGE 91

LESSON 8
Functions

Vocabulary   Topics of conversation
Function   Managing a conversation
Language to go   What to say in social situations

Nice to meet you

Vocabulary and speaking

1   **Look at the topics in the box. In pairs, discuss the following question.**

What topics of conversation do you think are appropriate when you meet someone for the first time?

> the football results   your love life   his / her salary
> your bad health   last night's TV programmes
> the weather   his / her good taste in clothes
> how much his / her haircut cost   a death in the family

Listening

2   **Look at the photo. In pairs, discuss the following questions.**

1   Which of the people know each other?
2   Which of the people are meeting for the first time?

3    **Listen to the first part of the conversation between Susie, Barry and Tom. Check your answers to Exercise 2.**

4   **Listen to the complete conversation. Are the statements true (T) or false (F)?**

1   Barry is American.
2   Tom prefers British weather.
3   Barry likes Susie's new suit.
4   Susie is taking a course at college.
5   Susie's mother likes Susie to be on time.
6   Barry would like to meet Susie again soon.

Language focus

5   **Look at the recording script on page 119 and find examples to complete the table.**

Functions	Examples
1 opening a conversation	
2 congratulating	*That's brilliant! Well done.*
3 introducing	
4 complimenting	
5 'making conversation'	
6 criticising	
7 closing a conversation	

Practice

6 **Put the words in the correct order to make sentences.**

Example: to Hi, you again. see lovely
Hi, lovely to see you again.

1 really the your I love of hair. colour
2 most at party! the beautiful the You're woman
3 me phoned for You ages! haven't
4 on birth of the baby! Congratulations your
5 to you my Can wife? I introduce
6 morning? news you the hear this Did
7 are you at How moment? getting the on
8 send Please to family. my your love
9 results are done! Well exam fantastic! Your
10 a it? It's day, lovely isn't

7 📼 **Listen to the sentences and check your answers to Exercise 6. Repeat the sentences with the correct pronunciation.**

Get talking ...

8 **Choose three of the functions in Exercise 5 and make up a short conversation for two or three people.**

1 In groups, practise the conversation aloud. Remember to think about the intonation.

2 Try repeating the conversation without your notes.

...and writing

9 **Write a similar conversation for three people using three different functions from Exercise 5.**

Language to go

A: Can I introduce you? Barry, this is Tom ...
  Tom, this is Barry.
B: Pleased to meet you, Tom.
C: Nice to meet you too, Barry.

> GRAMMAR REFERENCE PAGE 109
> PRACTICE PAGE 91

Vocabulary	Travel items
Grammar	First conditional
Language to go	Making suggestions to visitors to your area

Australia

Vocabulary and speaking

1 Match a word from the column on the left with one from the column on the right to make compound nouns. Then label the items.

water	cream
sleeping	boots
first-aid	belt
money	bag
mosquito	book
guide	clothes
sun	bottle
walking	repellent
rain	kit

2 In pairs, discuss the following questions.

Which of the things from Exercise 1 would you take on a ...
- two-week beach holiday?
- trip to the mountains?
- holiday to the middle of Australia?
- weekend visit to London?

Reading

3 Look at the photo opposite and discuss these questions about the Australian outback.

1 When is the best time to go?
2 What outdoor activities are there?
3 What wildlife can you see?
4 What's the best way to travel?
5 What health risks are there?
6 What art and culture is there?

4 Group A read the text below. Group B turn to page 84 and read the second part of the text.

1 Match each paragraph with the correct question from Exercise 3.
2 Check the answers to your questions.
3 Discuss your answers with a partner from the other group.

The Australian Outback

A _____

The outback is huge – it's 3,022 km from Adelaide to Darwin. So, unless you have a lot of time, you'll find flights and hire car are the best ways to travel. It'll be cheaper to buy a pass, if you plan several flights.

B _____

Unless you like extremely hot weather, avoid December and January when it can be 40°C. If you go in July and August, it won't be too hot, but the nights are freezing. The best times to visit are April to June and October to November.

3

6

Grammar focus

5 **Example A is the first conditional. Find other examples in the texts then complete the rules below.**

> A *If* you *go* in July and August, it *won't be* too hot.
> B *Unless* you *like* extremely hot weather, *avoid* December.

1 We usually use *if* + a verb in the _____ tense in one clause, and a modal verb in the other clause.
2 We use modal verbs like _____ , _____ or _____ .
3 *If* can sometimes be replaced with *unless*. Does *unless* mean *if* or *if not*?
4 What form is the verb *avoid* in Example B?

6 Listen and repeat the sentences.

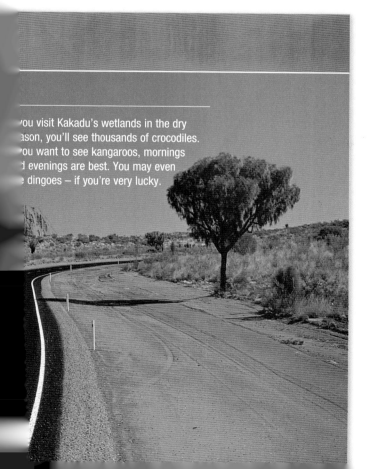

...you visit Kakadu's wetlands in the dry ...ason, you'll see thousands of crocodiles. ...ou want to see kangaroos, mornings ...d evenings are best. You may even ...e dingoes – if you're very lucky.

Practice

7 **Match the phrases to make first conditional sentences. Use *if*, *if not* or *unless*. There may be more than one answer.**

Example: *1-e You may see fantastic sunrises if you get up early.*

1 see fantastic sunrises
2 need to wear walking boots
3 take a water bottle

4 not need rain clothes
5 want to do canoeing
6 need to use sun cream
7 book in advance
8 have so much to carry

a) not get a ticket for the flights
b) travel light
c) find tour companies offering adventure sports
d) stay healthy
e) get up early
f) visit the mountains
g) get sunburn
h) go in the dry season

Get talking ...

8 **Think about your country, a region of your country or somewhere else that you know.**

1 Use the questions in Exercise 3 to help you make notes about your chosen place.
2 Work in pairs.
  Student A is a travel agent giving suggestions and information.
  Student B is a visitor asking questions.
3 Then change roles.

... and writing

9 **Write a short article for a travel magazine describing the place you talked about in Exercise 8.**

Language to go

A: When's the best time to go?
B: If you go in winter, you'll avoid the crowds.

> GRAMMAR REFERENCE PAGE 110
> PRACTICE PAGE 92

Vocabulary | Expressions with *take*
Grammar | Verb constructions for likes and dislikes
Language to go | Discussing sport

Take it easy

Vocabulary

> I can't stand studying any more. I'm going to *take it easy* instead.

> I don't mind helping if you've *taken on* too much work.

> Peter wasn't at the office today. He *took the day off.*

> I'm sick of this report. Just let me *take a break* for an hour.

> I'm really into getting fit so I'm *taking part in* this year's marathon.

> What's new? Well, I've *taken up* yoga. I'm really keen on it!

1 Write the expressions with *take* next to the correct definitions in the box.

Expression with *take*	Definition
1 take part in	participate in an activity
2	agree to do something
3	relax
4	begin something new
5	have a holiday from work
6	stop and have a rest

Listening and speaking

2 Look at the photo of Astra and Ian.

1 In pairs, describe what is happening.
2 Imagine what they are saying to each other.

3 📼 Listen to Astra and Ian's conversation and answer the following questions.

1 What reason does Ian give for not going to the gym?
2 What is Astra's reaction?
3 What is Ian's real reason?

Grammar focus

4 a) Look at the examples in the box and match the words in *italics* with the correct definition below.

A I can't stand *watching* football.
B You can *play* tennis tomorrow.
C I don't want *to go* running tonight.
D I'm keen on *aerobics*.

1 noun (or noun phrase)
2 the *-ing* form
3 infinitive with *to*
4 infinitive without *to*

b) Look back at Exercise 1 and the recording script for Exercise 3 on page 119 and find other ways of expressing likes and dislikes.

Expressing likes
But I thought you liked going?

Expressing dislikes
I can't stand studying

Notice what comes after each expression. Is it an *-ing* form, infinitive or noun (or noun phrase)?

Practice

5 Write sentences using the prompts. Make any necessary changes.

Example: I really / can't stand / go / running.
I really can't stand going running.

1 I / sick of / be unfit / so I / take up aerobics.
2 We enjoy / take / exercise / but we / like / take it easy / at other times.
3 It's quiet / 6.00 / so / I / not mind / get up early / go running.
4 You / keen on / get fit?
5 After / I / done / two hours' exercise / I / need / take / break.
6 They / love / watch / baseball on television.

6 ▭▭ Listen to the sentences and check your answers to Exercise 5. Repeat the sentences with the correct pronunciation.

Get talking

7 Compare opinions about sport.

1 Think about the following questions.
• Which sports were you most / least keen on when you were younger?
• Which sports are you most / least keen on now?
• Do you prefer team sports or individual sports?
• Have you taken up a new hobby or sport recently?
• Do you think some people take sport too seriously?

2 In groups, discuss your answers.

Language to go

A: Do you like taking part in team games?
B: No, I don't. I can't stand sport!

> GRAMMAR REFERENCE PAGE 110
> PRACTICE PAGE 92

Vocabulary	Determination
Grammar	*Used to* and *would*
Language to go	Comparing past and present habits

Determination

Vocabulary and speaking

1   In pairs, look at the picture and discuss the following questions.

  1 Where is this man?
  2 What is he doing?
  3 How do you think he feels about smoking, coffee and the Internet?

2   Complete the text below with the words in the box. Were your predictions in Exercise 1 correct?

> gave up   addict   addiction   willpower   quit
> determination   addicted   cut down   dependent

'My job is quite stressful, and you need a lot of **determination** to succeed. I often work late hours, and the coffee and cigarettes help to keep me awake. I know I should [1] _____ smoking but I've got very little [2] _____ . I [3] _____ three years ago, but a week later I started again. I'm probably a bit [4] _____ on cigarettes, and that worries me. I think I've got a bit of a coffee [5] _____ too, I drink it all the time. I love the taste though, so I don't even want to [6] _____ on that. The only other thing I'm [7] _____ to is the Internet. It fascinates me. I'm a real Web [8] _____ !'

3   In pairs, discuss the following questions.

  1 Are addictions always a bad thing?
  2 What things can be addictive?

Listening

4    Listen to four people talking about their addictions and habits. Complete the table.

Speaker	Addiction	Have they given up?	Details
1	Chocolate		
2			
3			
4			

Grammar focus

5 Look at the recording script on page 119 and complete the example sentences. Then answer the questions.

> A I _____ live alone.
> B I didn't _____ do much sport.
> C I'_____ have some chocolate before meals.
> D Did you _____ to smoke?

1 In example C, is *I'd* a contraction of *I had* or *I would*?
2 Are the examples in the box talking about a repeated action in the past, or a past state?
3 Complete the chart below. Tick (✓) if it is possible to use *used to* and *would*, and cross (✗) if it's not possible.

	used to	would
Single past action	✗	✗
Repeated past action		
Past state		

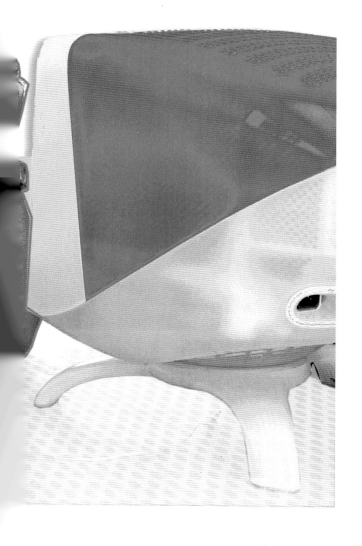

Practice

6 a) Rewrite the sentences so that they have the same meaning. Use the correct form of *used to* and the verbs in brackets.

Example: This time last year he smoked three packets a day. Now he doesn't smoke at all.
(smoke) **He used to smoke three packets a day.**

1 At school I hated sport. Now I'm addicted to it.
(hate) _____
2 He went to Italy every year when he was a child.
(go) _____
3 She never goes skiing now. Did she go skiing a lot before?
(go skiing?) _____
4 He didn't like computers. Now he's always on the Net.
(not like) _____
5 She doesn't bite her nails now. Did she bite them as a child?
(bite?) _____
6 I walked our dog every afternoon when I was younger.
(walk) _____

b) In which sentences could you also use *would*?

7 🔊 Listen and repeat the sentences with the correct pronunciation of *used to*.

Get talking

8 Discuss past habits.

1 Write a sentence to describe a 'naughty' or funny thing you used to do when you were younger. Give it to your teacher.

Example: **I used to knock on people's doors then run away.**

2 You will receive information about another student. Ask questions to find out who it is.

Example: **Did you use to ... ?**

Language to go

> A: Would you like a chocolate?
> B: No, thanks. I used to eat them, but not now!

> GRAMMAR REFERENCE PAGE 110
> PRACTICE PAGE 93

LESSON **12**
The present

Vocabulary — Money and banks
Grammar — Verbs with two objects
Language to go — Talking about money

Money matters

Vocabulary and speaking

1 **In pairs, look at the photos showing different ways of banking and discuss these questions.**

1 Do you use a bank? Why / Why not?
2 What do you use it for?
3 Which of these methods of banking do you prefer? Why?
4 What are the advantages and disadvantages of each method?

2 **Explain the differences in meaning between the pairs of expressions in the box below.**

borrow money / lend money

Example: You <u>borrow</u> money from a bank (or someone), and the bank (or someone) <u>lends</u> it to you.

> 1 invest money / save money
> 2 a bank account / a bank statement
> 3 a current account / a savings account
> 4 deposit money / withdraw money
> 5 receive interest / pay interest
> 6 be in the black / be in the red

3 **Look at the bank statement and answer the questions.**

1 What kind of account is it?
2 How much money did the customer deposit?
3 How much money did the customer withdraw?
4 Did the customer pay or receive interest?
5 Is the customer in the black or in the red?

● First-Class Bankers Direct   FCB**d**

Current account number: 8103391

Statement of account

Date		Paid out	Paid in	Balance
24 Aug	Balance brought forward			2,312.7
29 Aug	Blue Bird Café	17.50		2,295.2
06 Sep	Cheque 100476		150.00	2,445.2
15 Sep	Southern Electricity	43.50		2,401.7
21 Sep	Net interest to 20 Sep		14.52	2,416.3
22 Sep	Balance carried forward			2,416.3

Reading

4 **Read the text and decide if the sentences are true (T) or false (F).**

1 You can check your bank statement at any time.
2 You can't use your mobile phone to contact the bank.

3 You can borrow money from this bank.
4 You can get advice about shopping online.

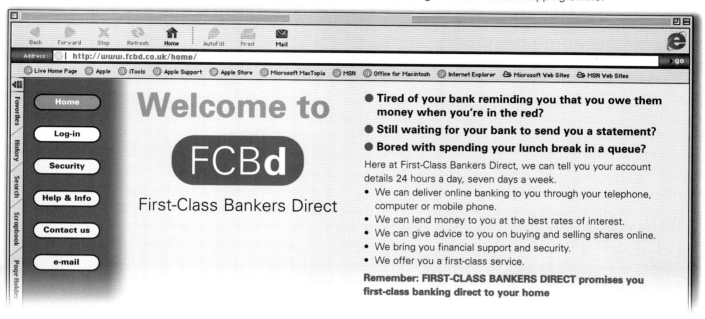

Welcome to FCBd
First-Class Bankers Direct

● **Tired of your bank reminding you that you owe them money when you're in the red?**
● **Still waiting for your bank to send you a statement?**
● **Bored with spending your lunch break in a queue?**

Here at First-Class Bankers Direct, we can tell you your account details 24 hours a day, seven days a week.

• We can deliver online banking to you through your telephone, computer or mobile phone.
• We can lend money to you at the best rates of interest.
• We can give advice to you on buying and selling shares online.
• We bring you financial support and security.
• We offer you a first-class service.

Remember: FIRST-CLASS BANKERS DIRECT promises you first-class banking direct to your home

Grammar focus

5 **Look at the examples in the box and answer the following questions.**

> A We *offer you a first-class service*.
> B We can *lend money to you*.

1 How many objects does each verb have?
2 What is the direct object in each sentence?
3 What is the indirect object?
4 Does *to* go with a direct or indirect object?
5 Does *to* + object go before or after the direct object?

6 **Find seven more similar verbs + objects in the text in Exercise 4.**

Practice

7 **Find the mistake in each of the sentences and correct it.**

Example: They will pay ~~to~~ you interest. ✗

1 We more choice promise you.
2 Would you like to tell anything?
3 A fantastic birthday present he gave me.
4 I can lend you the money to you.
5 When will you send to me the products?
6 You don't owe any money me.
7 We will deliver your shopping direct your home.

Get talking

8 **Congratulations! Your group has won first prize in the lottery and has to decide what to do with the money.**

1 First decide what you would do. These ideas may help you.
   • Buy presents for your friends (Who? What presents?)
   • Keep some for yourself (How much? Invest it?)
   • Lend some to a friend to start a business (How much? Receive interest?)
   • Give some to your family (How much?)
   • Give some to a charity (What charity? How much?)

2 In groups, talk about and compare your decisions.

Language to go

A: **Can you** lend me £10?
B: Sorry, **I never** lend money to friends!

> GRAMMAR REFERENCE PAGE 110
> PRACTICE PAGE 93

Vocabulary   Phrasal verbs about tourism
Grammar   Present simple and continuous for future
Language to go   Describing plans for a trip

The river

Vocabulary and speaking

1   Match the verbs in *italics* with the correct definitions.

Phrasal verbs	Definitions
1 They *set off* at 6.30 in the morning.	a) to continue
2 The car *broke down*, so I phoned the mechanic.	b) to give (someone) temporary accommodation
3 The tour *went on* for two hours.	c) to stop working (a machine)
4 We were tired of walking, so we *carried on* by bus.	d) to begin a journey
5 We'll *start off* in the High Street.	e) to finish part of a journey (by bus, train, boat etc.)
6 My friends *put me up* for two nights.	f) to begin a journey at a particular place
7 *Get off* the bus at the big supermarket. You can't miss it.	g) to last (time something takes)

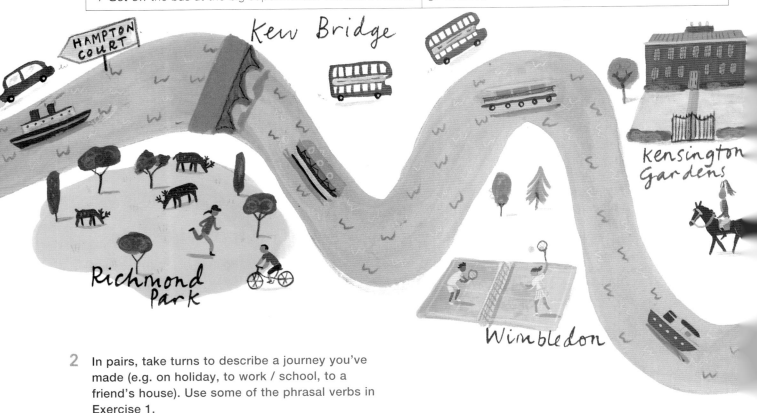

2   In pairs, take turns to describe a journey you've made (e.g. on holiday, to work / school, to a friend's house). Use some of the phrasal verbs in Exercise 1.

Listening

3   Look at the map of the River Thames in London. In pairs, discuss the following questions.

1 Which places do you know?
2 Have you been to London?
   If not, would you like to go?
3 If yes, did you visit any of the places on the map?

4   [icon] Listen to the conversation between a tourist and a travel agent.

Tick (✓) the places they mention on the map.

5   Listen again and answer the questions.

1 What time does the tour start?
2 What time do they arrive at the hotel?
3 What is the tourist doing on the first evening?
4 What is the tourist doing on the second evening?

Grammar focus

6 a) Look at the examples in the box opposite and say what tense is used for each.

> A The tour *starts* at 7.30 tomorrow.
> B I'*m meeting* a friend for dinner that evening.
> C What time *does* the boat *set off*?
> D I'*m going* to the theatre tonight.

b) Underline the correct alternatives and give examples to complete the rules.

1 We use the *present simple / present continuous* when we talk about itineraries, timetables or programmes.

   Example sentences: _____ and _____ .

2 We use the *present simple / present continuous* when we talk about more personal arrangements.

   Example sentences: _____ and _____ .

Practice

7 Complete the sentences using the correct form of the present simple or present continuous.

Example: What time **does the film start?** (the film / start)?

1 I _____ (finish) work at 4 o'clock on Fridays.
2 I _____ (meet) Daniel at the station at 10.30.
3 What _____ (you / do) this evening?
4 The museum tour _____ (start) at 11 a.m.
5 The school term _____ (finish) on 22nd July.
6 Mick _____ (come) to see us tomorrow.
7 When _____ (your college course / begin)?

Get talking

8 In groups, choose one of the following ideas for a day trip.

• A boat trip on a river   • A walking tour around a city

1 Plan your trip. Think about:
   a) The itinerary: the places the tour visits, how long the trip goes on, the start and finish times etc.
   b) Personal arrangements: things that people in your group are doing which are not included in the itinerary.

2 Tell the class about your itinerary and personal arrangements. Decide on the most interesting trip.

Language to go

A: What time does it start?
B: It starts at 9.00, but we're meeting at 8.30. Don't be late!

> GRAMMAR REFERENCE PAGE 110
> PRACTICE PAGE 94

Vocabulary 1   Weddings
Vocabulary 2   Uses of *get*
Language to go   Talking about relationships

Radio wedding

Vocabulary and speaking

1   **Look at these words about weddings and explain the difference between the pairs of words.**

1   bride / bridesmaid
2   groom / best man
3   fiancé / fiancée
4   religious ceremony / civil ceremony
5   reception / honeymoon

2   **In pairs, discuss these questions.**

1   How did your parents meet?
2   How long did your parents know each other before they got married?
3   How old were they when they got married?
4   What do you think about weddings?

Reading

3   **a) Carla and Greg (above) had a very unusual wedding. These things were all connected to it in some way.**

a radio station   a competition   the press

What do you think the connection is?

b) Work in groups. Group A: Turn to page 84. Group B: Turn to page 87.

Read your text and answer your questions.

4   **Talk to students from the other group. Tell them the information from your text.**

Vocabulary focus

5 Match the expressions in *italics* with the correct definitions.

Expressions	Definitions
1 Carla and Greg *got married* as a prize.	a) make someone annoyed
2 They didn't *get to know* each other first.	b) become sad and angry
3 She *gets on* my *nerves*.	c) end a marriage officially
4 They didn't *get engaged* first.	d) become husband and wife
5 Carla's mother *got upset* at the wedding.	e) become partners again
6 He'd like to *get back together* with Sue.	f) return to your usual state of happiness
7 They don't know if they'll *get on with* each other.	g) agree to get married
8 Greg *got divorced* from his first wife last year.	h) find out about each other
9 She hasn't *got over* her old boyfriend.	i) have a friendly relationship with (someone)

6 Divide the expressions with *get* in Exercise 5 into three groups.

get + adjective	*get* as a fixed expression	*get* as a phrasal verb
get married	get to know	

Practice

7 Complete the sentences with an expression with *get*. Remember to use the correct form of the verb.

Example: Amanda and Mick _got married_ last summer. She looked beautiful in her white dress.

1 After we split up, it took me two years _____ it.
2 He bites his nails all the time. It's so irritating – he really _____ .
3 It's important for people to _____ each other before they decide to get married.
4 Sometimes people _____ and have a party a year or so before they get married.
5 It's very sad – a high percentage of couples _____ .
6 She _____ when she saw her boyfriend with someone else.
7 My first wife and I _____ each other now – we are good friends.
8 My boyfriend and I split up in June – but we talked about things and now we are OK – in fact, we _____ three weeks ago.

Get talking ...

8 In groups, discuss the following questions.

1 Were Carla and Greg happy together? Why / Why not?
2 Forty per cent of marriages in the UK end in divorce. Why?
3 Arranged marriages never work. Do you agree?
4 What makes a good marriage?

... and writing

9 Write a letter to a friend telling them Carla and Greg's story, or news about a friend's relationship.

Language to go

A: Why did they get divorced?
B: They just didn't get on with each other.

> GRAMMAR REFERENCE PAGE 111
> PRACTICE PAGE 94

Vocabulary   *Waste, use, spend, save* + noun
Grammar   Modal verbs for giving advice
Language to go   Giving advice

Less is more

Vocabulary and speaking

1   **a) Look at the spidergram. It shows how the verb** *waste* **can go with these nouns.**

electricity / energy
paper
time
money
waste
opportunities
space
resources

b) Make spidergrams for the verbs *use*, *spend* **and** *save*. **Use the same nouns.**

Which verb + noun combinations are *not* typical?

2   **In pairs, look at the picture of the office. Make as many sentences as possible using verb + noun combinations from Exercise 1.**

Example: **They are wasting electricity because all the lights are on.**

3   **In pairs, discuss the following sentences and** <u>underline</u> **your answers.**

1 If you want to feel less tired, then you should sleep *more / less*.
2 If you want to be more effective in business, you should use technology *more / less*.
3 To be more successful at work, work *longer / shorter* hours.
4 You ought to eat *more / less* if you want to be healthier.

Listening

4 Read this text.

1 Where does it come from?
2 What do you think Laura Evans will say about each sentence in Exercise 3?

10.00 a.m. Life as it is!
This week's guest is Laura Evans, one of the US's top management consultants. She talks about the ideas behind her best-selling book *Less is really more!*

▶◀ Now listen to the radio programme and check your answers.

5 Listen again. Which advice do you agree with? Compare your ideas with a partner.

Grammar focus

6 Look at these different ways of giving advice and complete the rules below.

> A We *should work* shorter hours.
> B You *shouldn't forget* that technology is for saving energy, not wasting it.
> C Perhaps we *could try* it too?
> D You *ought to try* it.

1 In examples A, B and C, we use the modal verbs _____ and _____ .
2 After these modal verbs, we use _____ .
3 Example D is different because _____ .

Practice

7 Look at the sentences giving advice about going to sleep at night. Find the mistake in each sentence and correct it.

Example: You should ~~to~~ wear ear plugs. ✗

1 You could opening the window for more fresh air.
2 Perhaps you ought go bed earlier.
3 You don't should watch horror movies before going to bed.
4 Perhaps you must should do more exercise.
5 You should ought read a book in bed.
6 You should not to drink so much coffee.
7 Couldn't you to try drinking warm milk?

8 ▶◀ Listen and repeat the sentences.

Get talking…

9 Give advice to people who have got different kinds of problems.

1 Find out your problems.
   Student A: Turn to page 84.
   Student B: Turn to page 86.
   Student C: Turn to page 87.
2 Work in groups. Share your problems and give advice on what to do.

…and writing

10 Choose one of the problems and write a short letter to a friend giving him / her advice on that problem.

Language to go

A: What should I do?
B: You ought to relax more.

> GRAMMAR REFERENCE PAGE 111
> PRACTICE PAGE 95

LESSON 16
Connecting

Vocabulary The five senses
Grammar Defining relative clauses
Language to go Defining people, things, time and place

Looks good!

A

B

C

Vocabulary and speaking

1 Which of the senses in the box do you associate with each photo? Why?

| sight taste smell touch hearing |

2 a) In pairs, decide which photo goes with each sentence.

1 They *taste* delicious.
2 It *sounds like* the sea.
3 It *looks* really calm.
4 It *feels* very smooth.
5 It *looks like* a beautiful evening.
6 They *smell* very sweet.
7 It *sounds* strange.

b) When do we use *looks like* and *sounds like*?

Reading

3 In pairs, discuss this question.

How do you think smells like fresh bread, coconut or lemon can help businesses?

Read the advertisement opposite to see if you were correct.

4 Read the advertisement again and answer the questions.

1 Which part of our brains do smells go to?
2 Which places use the smell of fruit?
3 Which two smells make people feel relaxed?
4 How can smells help office workers?

Smells that work

It takes two seconds for a smell to enter your nose and travel to a part of the brain which controls memory and emotions.
You probably do not realise what is making you hungry or suddenly quite calm.

Smells nice! Banks and hotels pump fruit-fragrances into reception areas.
Supermarkets use smells such as bread to make you want to buy
Travel agencies use coconut oil fragrances to persuade customers to travel to places where sunshine is the main attraction.

Fragrances are calming A New York clinic that used the smell of vanilla found that patients who attended regularly reported a reduction in stress of 65%. Airlines put lavender smell in planes to calm people who are nervous.

Benefits for employees Japanese compan use lemon smells to increase energy during the working day and flower scents to improve concentration before and after lunch.

Could smells help your business?
If this is the idea you've been waiting for, then contact us today. Remember, this could be the d
when your business experiences the sweet smell of success. Fin
out about smells that work!

Telephone us on 0131 496 0000

Grammar focus

5 **Complete these sentences from the advertisement with the correct relative pronoun.**

> A ... a part of the brain _____ *controls memory*.
> B ... travel to places _____ *sunshine is the main attraction*.
> C ... do not realise _____ *is making you hungry or suddenly quite calm*.
> D This is the idea *(that) you've been waiting for*.

The parts in *italics* are defining relative clauses.
They tell us which person or thing the speaker means.
Find four more examples in the text.

6 **Match the relative pronouns in the box with the correct functions. There may be more than one answer.**

> a) that   b) when   c) where   d) which
> e) who   f) whose

1 to talk about places
2 to talk about people
3 to talk about time
4 to talk about things
5 to talk about people and their possessions

7 **Look at example D in Exercise 5 and choose the correct alternative in the following rule.**

We don't need to use a relative pronoun when we are talking about *the subject / the object* of a sentence.

Practice

8 **Combine two sentences to make one. Add a relative pronoun (if necessary) and make any other changes.**

Example: There's that girl. She looks like your little sister.
There's that girl *who* looks like your little sister.

1 You made me happy. You said you loved me.
2 Look at that guy. He is driving an old Chevrolet.
3 That's the woman. Her daughter plays the clarinet.
4 I loved the smell of the flowers. You sent them to me.
5 I don't like those nightclubs. They play techno there.
6 I love the quiet of the night. It's very calm and peaceful then.
7 Did you like the CD? I lent it to you.

Get talking

9 **How do you feel about each of the five senses?**

1 Think of your favourite thing for each of the five senses. Can you also think of things you hate?
2 In groups, discuss your choices.

Likes					
Dislikes					

Language to go

> A: I love the smell of bread which is still warm
> B: I prefer the taste!

> GRAMMAR REFERENCE PAGE 111
> PRACTICE PAGE 95

Vocabulary   Lifestyle: word building
Grammar   Present perfect simple with *yet, already, just*
Language to go   Describing recent changes

Changes

Vocabulary and speaking

1 **Which of these things do you have in your life at the moment?**

> happiness   good health   calm   success   stress
> good luck   noise   energy   wealth

2 **In pairs, discuss these questions about Exercise 1.**

1 Which things would you like to have more / less of?
2 Decide on the three most important.
3 What, if anything, can we do to change things?

Reading

3 **Read the article opposite about Feng Shui.**

1 Where does Feng Shui come from?
2 What does the article say you should do every day?
3 What does the article say about colours?

4 **Read the text again and find the adjectives that go with the nouns in Exercise 1.**

Example: **happiness (noun) – happy (adjective)**

36

Listening

5 [🔊] Listen to the radio programme. Tick (✓) the Feng Shui advice Graham has tried.

6 Listen again. Are these statements true (T) or false (F)?

1 He's recently started running.
2 He believes the fish have brought him good luck.
3 He thinks Feng Shui is a waste of time.
4 He's already tidied his workplace.

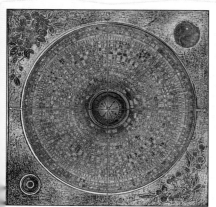

Chart used for setting up Feng Shui.

Want to change your life but don't know how?

Is Feng Shui the answer?

Feng Shui is an ancient Chinese philosophy for a healthy, happy and successful lifestyle. Read on for some advice ...

❏ Take up a sport or start going to the park every day. Make sure you get some fresh air during the day.
❏ Start your day with a glass of water, you'll feel more energetic.
❏ Buy a fish tank – fish are considered lucky, so you may even become wealthy!
❏ Tidy your home and workplace every day and put all your trash outside.
❏ Use plants to create a calm atmosphere at home or work.
❏ Stop wearing grey clothes. Grey is neither black nor white; it's a sign of confusion.
❏ Try to avoid stressful situations, like crowded streets and noisy traffic.

Remember: with Feng Shui, you don't predict the future, you change it.

Grammar focus

7 Look at the recording script on page 120 and complete the examples.

> A I've _____ *tried* one or two of the ideas.
> B *Have* you *bought* any fish _____ ?
> C I've _____ *bought* myself a new black suit.

8 Match *already*, *just* and *yet* with the following explanations.

1 something didn't happen, but you expect it to happen in the future: _____
2 something happened very recently: _____
3 something happened sooner than expected: _____
4 _____ always comes before the verb.
5 _____ always comes at the end of a clause.
6 _____ is not used in positive sentences.
7 _____ is not used in negative sentences.

Practice

9 Write sentences using the prompts. Make any necessary changes.

Example: Do you like the plants? Jane / buy them. (just)
Do you like the plants? Jane has just bought them.

1 Kumiko works really hard. She / do her homework. (already)
2 I hope everything is OK. Michael / not phone me. (yet)
3 My neighbour / rearrange / his living room. It looks great! (just)
4 A: Where are you going on holiday?
  B: I don't know – I / not decide. (yet)
5 Do you want to borrow this book about Feng Shui? I / finish it. (just)
6 A: Is Daniel still here?
  B: No, he / go. (already)
7 I work very fast. I / learn those English verbs. (already)
8 You know that film about China? You / see it? (yet)

Get talking

10 In groups, talk about changes in your lives.

Think about home, work, family, sport, hobbies, personal appearance.

1 What changes have you made recently?
2 What changes do you want to make, but haven't started yet?

Language to go

A: Have **you** moved in yet?
B: Yes, Mother, we've just arrived. No, you can't come for dinner!

> GRAMMAR REFERENCE PAGE 111
> PRACTICE PAGE 96

LESSON 18
Functions

Vocabulary Phrasal verbs: *turn, switch, go*
Function Informal and polite requests
Language to go Making and responding to requests

How polite are you?

Speaking and vocabulary

1 **In pairs, describe the noises in and around the room you are in.**

2 **Listen to these noises and say what they are. How do you feel about them?**

3 **In pairs discuss these questions.**

1 Are you a noisy person? If so, when?
2 How do you feel about other people's noise?

4 **Complete the sentences with a word from the box.**

off (x3) on (x2) down up over

1 I hate it when my alarm goes _____ in the morning.
2 I want to listen to that programme. Please turn the radio _____ .
3 As soon as he gets home, he switches _____ the TV and watches the evening news.
4 Please turn _____ all mobile phones in the aircraft.
5 Can we turn _____ to Channel 4, please? I want to watch that Italian film.
6 Please turn the radio _____ . I can't hear it very well.
7 Let's switch the TV _____ and have dinner in peace!
8 That music's too loud. Please turn it _____ .

Reading

5 **Work in pairs. Do the quiz for each other, then discuss your answers. Does your partner think you are polite? Is he / she right?**

Language focus

6 **Look at the answers in the quiz.**

1 Underline the different ways of making requests.
2 When you ask *Do you mind?* or *Would you mind?* the response *No*, means:
OK, it's no problem. or
It's not OK, there is a problem.

'Excuse me ...'

1 You're on a bus. The person next to you is playing loud music. What do you say?

A 'Would you mind turning your music down, please?'
B 'Excuse me, but I can't read my book with all that noise.'
C 'You're very rude, aren't you?'

2 You're in class. The student behind you is kicking your chair. What do you say?

A 'Can you stop that, I can't concentrate.'
B 'Teacher! He's kicking my chair!'
C 'Stop that now!'

3 It's the middle of the night. Your neighbour's dog is barking. You can't sleep. Do you ...

A phone your neighbour and say 'Could you stop Mitzy barking, please?'
B phone the police and say 'Would you come quickly, there's a dangerous animal at Number 22!'
C open the window and shout 'SHUT UP!'

4 You're having a romantic dinner in a restaurant. A man near you is shouting on his mobile phone. What do you say?

A 'Do you mind moving somewhere else?'
B 'Waiter! Please tell this man to go outside.'
C 'I'm sorry, but we're trying to be romantic here!'

7 **Look at the requests and responses and say which is the most formal / most informal.**

1 A: *Could you* turn down your music?
B: Yes, of course. Sorry.

2 A: *Would you mind* turning your music down, please?
B: No, of course not.

3 A: *Turn* the music down a bit.
B: OK.

4 A: *Do you mind if* I turn my music on?
B: Not at all.

Now listen and repeat the requests and responses. Use polite intonation.

Practice

8 **Look at the pictures and write requests and responses for each situation.**

Example: Would you mind making less noise, please?
No, of course not.

1 _____

3 _____

2 _____

Get talking

9 **In pairs, prepare and practise short dialogues making and responding to requests.**

Student A: Turn to page 85.
Student B: Turn to page 86.

4 _____

Language to go

A: Could you turn **your music** down?
B: What did you say?
A: Would you mind turning **it** down?
B: No. Of course not.

> GRAMMAR REFERENCE PAGE 112
> PRACTICE PAGE 96

Vocabulary   Adjectives describing loneliness and fear
Grammar   Second conditional
Language to go   Talking about hypothetical situations

Going alone

100 days at sea

At the age of 24, Ellen MacArthur became the youngest and the smallest (she is only 1.57m) competitor to take part in the Vendée Globe race – the biggest challenge in sailing: 100 days alone.

Imagine how it would feel sailing single-handed, non-stop and unaided around the world. Not seeing another person for weeks on end, not knowing when a hurricane could hit your boat and end your chances of finishing, or even surviving.

To sail the roughest seas alone you need great ability and strength – Ellen has both. She remembers everything she reads and hears. 'You need so many different skills,' says Ellen. 'Alone at sea, you are a sailor, an electrician, an engineer and a cook. There is so much to do so that you never feel lonely. I wouldn't do it if I was scared of being alone.'

In order to avoid tiredness, Ellen trained to sleep for as little as twenty minutes at a time. 'Normal sleep is impossible: I slept for about four hours a day. If you needed more sleep, you could never finish the race.'

During her incredible voyage, she battled against ocean storms, not enough sleep and 23 much more experienced competitors, who were mostly men. By the force of her character Ellen eventually took second place and started a legend.

Vocabulary and speaking

1   **What is the difference between the words in *italics* in each group?**

1   a) When my girlfriend is away, I feel very *lonely* and really miss her.
b) I like living *alone*, because I can do whatever I want.

2   a) His mother is ill and he's very *worried* about her.
b) My children are *scared* of the dark, so we leave a light on at night.
c) I couldn't sleep because I was so *nervous* about the interview.

2   **In pairs, discuss the following questions.**

How do you feel about being ...
alone?   in the dark?   on an aeroplane?   in a very small space?

Reading

3   **Look at the photo and discuss the following questions.**

1   Where is this woman?
2   What is she doing?
3   How do you think she is feeling?

4   **Read the text to see if your ideas were correct.**

Grammar focus

6 Look at the examples of the second conditional in the box.
Then complete the rules below.

> A I *wouldn't do* it *if* I *was* afraid of being alone.
> B *If* you *needed* more sleep, you *could never finish* the race.

1 We use the second conditional to talk about *likely* or
unlikely / hypothetical situations.
2 a) We form the second conditional with *If* + _____ / *would ('d)* +
_____ .

   b) If you are less certain, you can use *might* or *could* (instead of
_____).

Practice

7 Rewrite these sentences using the second conditional.
Make any necessary changes.

Example: It's too cold. I probably won't go swimming.
If it wasn't so cold, I'd go swimming.

1 I miss other people too much. I don't want to take part in the race.
2 He doesn't go out much. He doesn't know many people.
3 I want to phone him. I don't know his number.
4 John isn't here. I want to ask him about the weekend.
5 I'm scared of small spaces. I want to use the lift.
6 People don't always understand me. I don't speak English very well.

8  Listen and repeat the sentences with the correct pronunciation.

Get talking

9 Imagine being alone for 100 days in one of these situations:

• a single-handed yacht race
• on a desert island

In groups, discuss the following questions.

1 How would you feel?
2 What five 'luxuries' would you take with you?

5 **Read the text again. Are the sentences true (T) or false (F)?**

1 Nobody can help the sailors during the race.
2 Ellen is afraid of being alone.
3 During the race, Ellen had little sleep.
4 Ellen was one of the most experienced competitors in the race.
5 She came second, so she wasn't very successful.

Language to go

A: If you went to a desert island,
what would you take?
B: I'd get very lonely, so I think I'd
take a friend!

> GRAMMAR REFERENCE PAGE 112
> PRACTICE PAGE 97

Vocabulary   Food and cooking
Grammar   Verb constructions with -ing / infinitive
Language to go   Talking about food and cooking

What's in the fridge?

Vocabulary and speaking

1   What is the difference between these words?

1   cook / chef / cooker
2   fridge / frozen / freezer
3   meal / course / plate
4   fast food / raw food / fresh food
5   boil / roast / fry
6   knife / fork / spoon
7   vegetable / vegetarian / vegan

2   In pairs, discuss the following questions.

1   What did you eat for lunch yesterday?
2   Where did you eat it?
3   Who cooked it? Was it nice?
4   What's in your fridge at the moment?

Listening

3   Look at the photos of two top chefs at home.

1   What do you think is in Takanori's fridge?
2   What do you think is in Gabriela's fridge?

4    Listen to the chefs and check your answers.

5   Listen again. Are the sentences true (T) or false (F)?

Takanori
1   He manages to keep his fridge tidy and organised.
2   He only keeps Japanese food in his fridge.
3   He spends time learning about different food.
4   He likes going out to Chinese restaurants with his friends.

Gabriela
5   She manages to keep her fridge tidy and organised.
6   She doesn't keep any beer in her fridge.
7   She often cooks pasta for visitors.
8   She likes going out to Italian restaurants with her friends.

Takanori Kotani from Japan

Grammar focus

6 **Look at the examples in the box. Then <u>underline</u> the correct alternatives in the rules below.**

> A I*'ve decided to visit* some other countries.
> B I *avoid cooking* complicated dishes at home.

1 In example A, *decide* is followed by *the -ing form / the infinitive*.
2 In example B, *avoid* is followed by *the -ing form / the infinitive*.

7 **Look at the recording script on page 120 and find examples with the verbs in the box.**

> plan   afford   waste time   spend time   give up
> keep on   avoid   offer   decide   manage

Is each verb followed by an *-ing* form or an *infinitive*?

Gabriela Bellini from Italy

Practice

8 **Complete the sentences using the correct form of the verbs in brackets.**

Example: I've got a new cook book, so I'm planning <u>*to do*</u> (do) more cooking in future.

1 Have you decided _____ (eat) at home or go out instead?
2 She's lost weight because she's given up _____ (eat) so much chocolate.
3 Even though we'd love to, we just can't afford _____ (eat) out every night.
4 I don't waste time _____ (read) recipes, I prefer my own ideas.
5 She offered _____ (do) the cooking as long as I did the dishes.
6 I'm going to avoid _____ (go) to that restaurant again; the service was terrible.
7 At the weekends, we spend time _____ (shop) and _____ (cook) exotic meals.
8 I'm going to learn to cook. I can't keep on _____ (buy) ready-made meals.
9 Did you manage _____ (find) that wine you were looking for?

Get talking

9 **In groups, discuss the following questions about the food you like cooking and eating. Try to use the verbs from Exercise 7.**

1 Who usually cooks in your house?
2 What kind of food do you like cooking / eating?
3 How often do you decide to go out for a meal?
4 How much time do you spend cooking?
5 Have you ever offered to cook a meal for more than ten people?
6 Is there anything you try to (or have to) avoid eating?
7 What do you think about your national dishes?
8 Do you like to try dishes from other countries?

Language to go

> A: Do you spend much time cooking?
> B: No, not cooking, just eating!

> GRAMMAR REFERENCE PAGE 112
> PRACTICE PAGE 97

Vocabulary Travel and airports
Grammar Past perfect simple
Language to go Recounting events in your life

Airport

Vocabulary and speaking

1 **Complete the sentences using the words in the box.**

| trip flight journey travel tour cruise |

1 The plane was very comfortable, and we had a lovely _____ .
2 I'm going on a short business _____ to New York next week.
3 My _____ to work is about 30 minutes.
4 We had a very good guided _____ round the museum.
5 Our car was stolen, so we had to _____ by train.
6 We went on a _____ around the Greek islands last year.

2 **Match the words in the box with the labelled items in the picture.**

a) cabin crew	e) flight-information screens
b) check-in desk	f) hand luggage
c) departure lounge	g) passport control
d) duty-free shops	h) boarding card

3 **In pairs, discuss the following questions.**

1 Do you enjoy travelling by plane? Why/Why not?
2 What problems sometimes happen at airports?
3 What do you think would make air travel better?

Reading

4 **Read the text quickly and answer this question.**

Did the traveller have a positive or negative experience in the airport?

5 **Read the text again. Are the sentences true (T) or false (F)?**

1 You land at a 'hub' to catch another plane.
2 It is easy to go to the wrong gate.
3 The man realised he had forgotten his book when he got on the plane.
4 When he went back, he couldn't find the book.
5 He got lost in the airport.

The Hub

Sometimes, you fly, not to your destination, but to a 'hub'. In other words, you fly to an airport to catch a plane to fly to another airport. You are in transit. You sit in a big room where all the seats are facing in the same direction, like the seats in a theatre. But there is no show. There is nothing.

You begin to feel ill. You do not know what time it is. In many airports, each terminal is the same as every other terminal. The corridors are the same as each other. But gate 36 may be hundreds of metres from gate 35, in any direction; it's easy to make a mistake.

I was once at Zurich airport. The weather was bad and the plane was delayed. I was drinking coffee at a bar and reading a book. Outside, the weather had got worse. Time passed. When the flight was called, I picked up my bags and moved towards the gate. I went down a corridor, down some steps, along a bit, down a bit. Then, just as I got to the gate, I realised I had left my book in the bar.

I tried to remember the route I had taken so I could do it in reverse. I was successful. The book was still there. Then I started running back. I ran down staircases, along corridors. I ran past a shop selling magazines. At some point, I knew that I had taken the wrong turn. At another point, I panicked.

Adapted from *The Observer* newspaper

Practice

7 Complete the sentences using the correct form of the past perfect simple or the past simple.

Example: When I _arrived_ (arrive) at the airport, the flight _had already left_ (already left).

1 We really _____ (want) a swim but we _____ (not / pack) our swimsuits.
2 I _____ (decide) to see the movie because I _____ (enjoy) the book so much.
3 As soon as I saw Rita, I _____ (realise) I _____ (meet) her before.
4 After Marek _____ (finish) his homework, he _____ (go) out with some friends.
5 When she _____ (ask) to see my boarding card, I realised I _____ (lose) it.
6 I knew I _____ (not / study) enough as soon as I _____ (see) the exam question.

8 🎧 **Listen and check your answers. Repeat the sentences with the correct pronunciation.**

Get talking ...

9 **Tell a story about a personal experience.**

1 Think of something interesting / important that happened to you. It could be about travel, your family, your job or something else.
2 Decide on seven key words / events in the story. Write them in boxes in the order they happened.
3 In pairs, tell the story of your experience. Start at number four (in the past). For things that happened before then, use the past perfect simple.

... and writing

10 **Write your story.**

Grammar focus

6 **Look at the example of the past perfect simple and then complete the rules.**

I realised I *had left* the book in the bar.

left book		now
	realised	

1 We use the past perfect simple to talk about an action that happened *before / after* another action in the past.
2 We form the past perfect simple with *had* + _____ .

Language to go

A: Did you ever see her again?
B: No. When I arrived, her flight had already left.

> GRAMMAR REFERENCE PAGE 112
> PRACTICE PAGE 98

Vocabulary   Fame and success
Grammar   Passive constructions
Language to go   Describing a process

A star is born... or made?

Vocabulary and speaking

1   **Look at the photos of famous people. In pairs, discuss the following questions.**

Why are / were they famous?
Would you like to meet them?

2   **Read some opinions expressed about the stars. Do you agree with them?**

1   I feel sorry for child stars like Macaulay Culkin who become so *famous* at an early age. They must find it hard to make any real friends.

2   The Spice Girls were very *fashionable* in the 1990s, and very *successful*. A lot of people thought they were amazing, but I didn't think they were very *talented* – they couldn't sing very well, for example.

3   Venus Williams is a *brilliant* tennis player, but I don't think she's as *skilful* as Navratilova was – she won Wimbledon nine times. That's what I call *legendary*!

4   Oasis were very *popular* and they sold millions of records, but I don't think they were very *original*. They sounded just like the Beatles to me!

3   **Look at the adjectives in *italics* in Exercise 2. Write down the nouns which the adjectives come from.**

Example: *famous [adjective] – fame [noun]*

Listening

4   **Read the radio programmes guide and think about the question in the first sentence. In pairs, discuss your answers.**

9.05pm **A Star is born ... or made?**
Are you born a star, do you become one or does someone make you a star? Listen to the story of the Spice Girls and make up your own mind! Presented by Philip Graham.
9.30pm **Sportsnight**

5   **Listen to the radio programme and find out the presenter's answer to the question.**

6   **Listen again. Are these statements true (T) or false (F)?**

1   A businessman created the Spice Girls in 1994.
2   At first, six Spice Girls were chosen.
3   Their first single wasn't a success.
4   Ginger Spice left the band to work for the United Nations.
5   One of the Spice Girls is married to a footballer.

Grammar focus

7 **Look at the examples in the box then complete the rules with *active* or *passive*.**

> **Active**
>
> | SUBJECT | VERB | OBJECT |
> | --- | --- | --- |
> | Businessmen | create | pop groups. |
>
> **Passive**
>
> | SUBJECT | VERB | THE PERSON OR THING THAT DOES IT |
> | --- | --- | --- |
> | Pop groups | *are created* | by businessmen. |

1 In _____ constructions, the subject is not the person or thing that does the action.
2 In _____ constructions, the subject is the person or thing that does the action.
3 _____ constructions are used:
   a) when we are talking about processes (e.g. making someone into a star).
   b) in more formal contexts.
   c) when the person or thing (the agent) is unknown or not important.

8 <u>Underline</u> the correct alternative to show how the passive is made.

be/have/do in the correct tense + the *infinitive/ past participle* of the main verb.

Practice

9 **Rewrite these sentences in the passive. Is the agent always needed?**

Example: The director asked the actress to audition for the part of Cleopatra.
The actress was asked to audition for the part of Cleopatra. [Agent not needed.]

1 The record company released the brilliant album *Skill* last year.
2 A journalist from *Time* magazine interviewed the new president.
3 The organisers always invite different celebrities to present the film awards.
4 They need two children for the TV show, 'Fun House'.
5 They announce the winning lottery numbers every Saturday.
6 The dance instructor teaches the singers how to dance.
7 Shops sold 10,000 tickets for the concert in an hour.

Get talking

10 **In pairs, ask and answer questions to complete information about the Williams sisters.**

Student A: Turn to page 85.
Student B: Turn to page 87.

Language to go

A: How did the audition go?
B: Really well, in fact I was chosen.
A: Congratulations!

> GRAMMAR REFERENCE PAGE 113
> PRACTICE PAGE 98

Vocabulary   Toys and games
Grammar   Modal verbs to talk about future probability
Language to go   Making predictions about the future

The future of toys

Vocabulary and speaking

1 Label the photos using the words in the box.

a) board game	b) computer game
c) jigsaw puzzle	d) construction kit
e) cards	f) skateboard
g) dolls	

2 In pairs, discuss the following questions.

1 Which toys and games did you play with when you were a child?
2 Which toys and games are popular with adults?
What about you?
3 What sort of toys do you think there will be in the future?

Reading

3 Read the text quickly to see if your ideas in Exercise 2 were similar.

4 Read the text again. Are these sentences true (T) or false (F)?

1 Some toys will protect children from traffic dangers.
2 Some toys may smell good.
3 Some toys will teach us new languages.
4 Children may be able to tell Ludic Robots what to do.
5 Footballs of the future might cause arguments.

Tomorrow's TOYS

In the future, toys will give us excitement, entertainment and wonderful learning opportunities. What sort of toys can we expect to see?

The Navigator Game® will connect to a child's bicycle. It will use technology to link children together and allow them to play simple games, such as hide-and-seek. The radio signal will also warn children of the danger of nearby cars.

Grammar focus

5 Look at the text again and complete the sentences in the box.

> A *The Navigator Game* ® _____ *connect* to a child's bicycle.
> B It _____ *be done* in many ways.
> C The Globe _____ *be used* as a nightlight.
> D Footballs of the future _____ *contain* video cameras.

6 Complete the rules.

1 When we think something is *very probable* in the future, we use _____ .
2 When we think the future is *less probable* (but still possible), we use _____ , _____ and _____ .
3 All the modal verbs are followed by _____ .

To show that the predictions are our opinions, we can use the following phrases.

I think ... *I expect ...*	followed by a phrase with *will*, *may*, *might* or *could*.
I'm sure ... *I don't think ...* *I doubt if ...*	followed by a phrase with *will*.

Emotional Communicators® will allow us to communicate love to family or friends. It may be done in many ways: sounds, pictures, smells, colour or by touch. We will receive these 'messages' on a necklace.

The Interactive Globe® will show us lots of information such as different time zones or examples of the world's languages. When not in use, the Globe could be used as a nightlight.

Ludic Robots® are small, electronic friends which respond to instructions. They can also be taught to do simple tasks, so children may become very fond of them.

Footballs of the future might contain video cameras. These cameras could show exactly where the ball is, so arguments about goals might become a thing of the past.

Practice

7 a) Put the words in the correct order to make sentences.

Example: will / computer / think / definitely / graphics / I / more / become / realistic
I think computer graphics will definitely become more realistic.

1 possible / expect / soon / will / I / to connect / it / computers / to / Lego® / be / models
2 have / Skateboards / motors / soon / electric / could
3 available / Personal / flying / the year 2015 / might / be / machines / by
4 people / computer / may / become / games / characters / Famous / in
5 I / if / teddy bears / people / buy / will / with / computers / them / doubt / inside
6 will / most / I / before / phones / long / children / have / mobile / think
7 don't / books / people / read / I / much / longer / paper / think / will / for
8 in / Children / be / unfit / the / might / very / future

b) Which sentences do you agree with?

Get talking ...

8 What are your opinions about the future of these things?

- toys and games
- cars and transport
- multi-media equipment
- clothes

1 Think about your own opinions.
2 In groups, discuss and compare your opinions.

... and writing

9 Choose one of the topics you talked about and write part of a catalogue describing some of the products that you predicted.

> GRAMMAR REFERENCE PAGE 113
> PRACTICE PAGE 99

LESSON **24**
Vocabulary

Vocabulary 1   Telephoning expressions
Vocabulary 2   Phrasal verbs about telephoning
Language to go   Communicating by phone

I'll call you

Speaking and vocabulary

1   **In pairs, discuss the following questions.**

1   Have you got a *mobile phone*? If so, when do you use it?
2   How many *calls do you make* per day / week?
3   What do you usually say when you *answer the phone*?
4   Do you ever have to use English *on the phone*? How does it feel?
5   How do you feel about *leaving a message* on an *answerphone*?
6   Do you ever make calls from a *pay phone*?
7   Do you like *texting* people?

2   **a) Look at these telephoning expressions and** <u>underline</u> **the correct word(s) to complete the sentences.**

1   Can I *give / leave* a message, please?
2   *I am / This is* Donna speaking.
3   The line's *occupied / busy* at the moment.
4   I'm *afraid / frightened* Mr Barnes isn't here at the moment.
5   *I like / I'd like* to speak to Jon Barnes, please.
6   *I'm / It's* Georgia King speaking.
7   Good morning, Barnes Johnson, for Sales *push / press* one.
8   I'm *replying / returning* his call.

b) Put the expressions in the order you might hear them in a telephone conversation.

Listening

3  Listen to the first part of the phone conversation and check your answers to Exercise 2b.

4 Now listen to the whole conversation and answer the questions.

1 Who does Georgia speak to first?
2 What is the problem?
3 What is the solution to the problem?
4 Who does Georgia speak to next?
5 Who does Georgia speak to last?

Vocabulary focus

5 Match the phrasal verbs (A–D) with the correct definitions (1–4).

A call someone back	1 connect somebody by telephone
B hang up	2 return a telephone call
C hold on	3 wait (on the telephone)
D put someone through	4 finish a telephone conversation

Now look at the recording script on page 121 and find an example sentence for each phrasal verb.

6 Underline the correct alternatives.

1 Can you ask him to *call back me / call me back*?
2 *Hold on / Hold you on* a minute, please.
3 I'm going to *hang up / hang you up* now.
4 I'll *put through you / put you through* to the office.

Practice

7 Correct the mistakes in the sentences below.

Example: If you want reception, ~~push~~ one. ✗ press

1 Give me Michael, please.
2 The line is occupied.
3 I'm extremely sorry that she's not here at the moment.
4 Please can you wait on the line.
5 I'll just put through you.
6 Do you want me to tell him something?
7 I am replying her earlier telephone call.
8 Could you try to speak to her again later?
9 I am me!

8 Listen and check your answers. Repeat the sentences with the correct pronunciation.

Get talking

9 In pairs, practise talking on the telephone.

Turn to page 85 for the situations.

1 Practise both the phone calls using the prompts.
2 Change roles and practise them again.
3 Now work with a different partner. Practise the phone calls but without the prompts.

Language to go

A: Hello, this is **Mark Smith** speaking. Can I speak to **Katy Jones**, please?
B: Yes, I'll just put you through.

> GRAMMAR REFERENCE PAGE 113
> PRACTICE PAGE 99

Vocabulary *Make* and *do*
Grammar Modal verbs for necessity and obligation
Language to go Describing rules in the present

Do the right thing

Vocabulary and speaking

1 The rules of social or professional behaviour are called etiquette. In pairs, discuss the following questions.

1 What do you take when you're invited for dinner: flowers, chocolates, a bottle of wine or something else?
2 What is appropriate to talk about in a social situation with work colleagues: the weather, politics, your family or something else?
3 How strict is the social and business etiquette in your country?
4 Describe a time when you *didn't* do the right thing.

2 Complete the sentences using *do* or *make*.

1 It's not important to _____ a good impression when you e-mail at work.
2 If you are unsure what to _____ , then _____ your e-mail more formal.
3 You should _____ your best to write long messages.
4 Use capital letters and exclamation marks when you want to _____ an important point.
5 Every e-mail address is different so _____ sure you check the address.

Now divide the expressions into two columns. Can you add any more to the list?

Expressions with *do*	Expressions with *make*
do (your) best	

Reading

3 In pairs, discuss the following question.

What do you think *Netiquette* means?

Look again at the sentences in Exercise 2. Do you think they are true (T) or false (F)?

4 Read the text to see if your answers about *Netiquette* were correct.

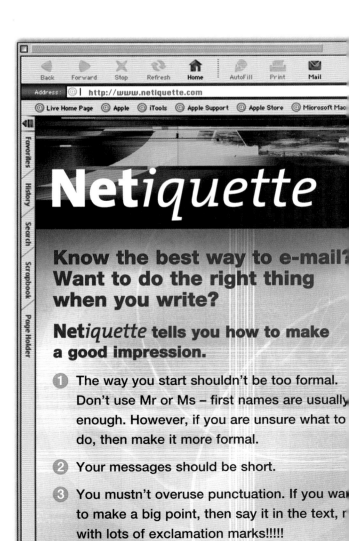

Netiquette

Know the best way to e-mail?
Want to do the right thing when you write?

Net*iquette* tells you how to make a good impression.

1 The way you start shouldn't be too formal. Don't use Mr or Ms – first names are usually enough. However, if you are unsure what to do, then make it more formal.

2 Your messages should be short.

3 You mustn't overuse punctuation. If you war to make a big point, then say it in the text, r with lots of exclamation marks!!!!!

Grammar focus

5 The verbs below are used to express obligation and necessity. Find one example from the text for each of the verbs.

Verb	Example from text
must	I must make it plain and simple.
mustn't	
have to	
don't have to	
should	
shouldn't	

6 Match the explanations below with the verbs in Exercise 5.

1 It's necessary (I'm telling myself): <u>must</u>
2 It's necessary (somebody else is telling me):
   _____
3 It's not a good idea: _____
4 It's not necessary: _____
5 It's prohibited/forbidden: _____
6 It's a good idea: _____

You don't have to use abbreviations, but they are great fun when writing to friends. For example, 'RUOK' means 'Are you OK?' and 'CU L8ER 2NITE' means 'See you later tonight'.

Facial expressions and body gestures are important in conversations. So if you want to show your emotions, use 'smilies' or 'emoticons'. A winking face is ;-)

You mustn't send an e-mail all in capital letters; IT'S LIKE SHOUTING IN SOMEONE'S EAR!

You have to use plain English. Tell yourself – 'I must make it plain and simple'.

Practice

7 Complete the sentences with the most appropriate verb. There may be more than one answer.

Example: When my computer crashes, I <u>have to</u> restart it.

1 Next Monday is a public holiday, so I _____ go to work.
2 Football players _____ touch the ball with their hands.
3 When you enter a country, you usually _____ show your passport.
4 You don't phone your mother much. I think you _____ phone her more.
5 I can't type very fast – I really _____ practise more.
6 You _____ wear a tie for the office, but you can if you want.
7 People _____ use mobile phones when they are driving. It's really dangerous.

Get talking ...

8 In pairs, discuss the 'rules' of behaviour for the following situations.

A You're going out for dinner with your new boss.
B You're meeting your girlfriend's / boyfriend's parents for the first time.

Think about ...
• what time to arrive / leave
• good / bad conversation topics
• what to wear / not to wear
• what to take / not to take
• what food / drink to have

... and writing

9 Write an e-mail to another pair of students telling them what to do / not to do for the situations you discussed in Exercise 8.

Language to go

A: What's the right thing to do?
B: You should do what you feel comfortable with.

> GRAMMAR REFERENCE PAGE 113
> PRACTICE PAGE 100

Vocabulary   Expressions with *time*
Grammar   Ways to express contrasting ideas
Language to go   Comparing attitudes

Six and a half hours

Vocabulary and speaking

1   **Match the halves of sentences to make expressions with *time*.**

1 His journey to work *takes* …	a) *the time* he gets home.
2 He is never late because …	b) *time off.*
3 He always arrives at work *on* …	c) *of time.*
4 He thinks commuting is *a waste* …	d) *a long time.*
5 He always feels stressed *by* …	e) *more time* with his family.
6 He would like to *spend* …	f) *time.*
7 He gets a lot of …	g) the journey is carefully *timed.*

Now think about your journey to work / school. Which of the sentences above are true for you?

2   **Tadao Masuda lives in Japan and commutes to work by train. In pairs, read the sentences in Exercise 1a again. Do you think they are true (T) or false (F) for him?**

Reading

3   **Read the text and check your answers to Exercise 2.**

4   **Read the text again and answer the questions.**

1   How long does he spend travelling each day?
2   How long is Tadao away from home each day?
3   How does he feel about the time on the train?
4   What special qualities does Tadao have?
5   Do you think Tadao will enjoy his retirement? Why / Why not?

Long-distance commuter

So you think you have a difficult journey to work; traffic, heat and other people. You fight through crowds, down tunnels, up escalators. And you arrive at work sweaty and tired. However, it could be a lot worse.

Consider Tadao Masuda who lives in Japan. His journey to work takes three and a quarter hours and then another three and a quarter back home again. He gets up at 4.00 a.m. Although he knows the journey time to the minute, he leaves nothing to chance. He sets off at 4.55, gets the train at 5.16 and always arrives at the office on time. He finally returns home at 8.50 in the evening. He knows his routine well – after all, he has done it for 30 years.

'I don't actually enjoy my commuting, but I definitely don't feel it is a waste of time. I use the time for my own thoughts. It is my private space. Despite many problems at work during the day, I've always forgotten them by the time I get home. It is my way of getting rid of stress.' Tadao is prepared to work hard. Despite not enjoying the journey, he does not complain about it.

Today at 65, he is considering a change. He would like to spend more time with his wife and family. In spite of staying with the same company all his life, he still only gets ten days off a year. However, will he be happy when he retires and ends his 30-year routine?

Grammar focus

5 All the words in *italics* in the box are ways of expressing contrasting ideas. Write one example from the text for each of the words.

6 Look at the position of the commas in the sentences. How do they affect pronunciation?

Now listen and repeat the sentences.

> A You arrive at work tired. *However*, it could be a lot worse.
> B *Although...*
> C *Despite...*
> D *Despite not...*
> E *In spite of...*

Practice

7 Rewrite the following sentences using the words in brackets. Make any necessary changes.

Example: My journey is long. I enjoy it. (although)
Although my journey is long, I enjoy it.

1 I like work. I don't like commuting. (although)
2 I don't really like my job. I need the money. (however)
3 She works hard all week. She takes it easy on Sundays. (although)
4 He is very busy. He manages to take some time off. (despite)
5 I leave on time. I'm always late. (in spite of)
6 He doesn't have an alarm clock. He always wakes up on time. (despite not)
7 Vocabulary is not easy to remember. It is essential. (however)
8 English verbs are easy. I have problems remembering the irregular ones. (in spite of)
9 I want to learn English. I don't do any homework. (despite)
10 I enjoy my English lessons. I'm often tired. (although)

Get talking...

8 Look again at the sentences in Exercise 7 and tick (✓) the ones that are true for you. If they are not true, think about what is and give examples.

In pairs, discuss your answers and compare your attitudes towards...
• work / school • being on time • learning English

... and writing

9 Write a letter to your boss apologising for being late for an important meeting and explaining your reasons.

Language to go

A: Are you usually on time?
B: Although I try to be on time, I'm often late.

> GRAMMAR REFERENCE PAGE 113
> PRACTICE PAGE 100

LESSON **27**
The perfect

Vocabulary Achievements and projects
Grammar Present perfect simple and continuous
Language to go Discussing personal achievements and projects

Achievement

Vocabulary and speaking

1 Match the verbs with the correct nouns to make expressions to do with achievements.

Verbs	Nouns
1 win	a) an ambition
2 pass	b) a certificate
3 receive	c) a race
4 invent	d) an exam
5 solve	e) a machine / device
6 achieve	f) a problem

In pairs, discuss the expression which you think is the most important in people's lives.

2 Complete the sentences with the words in the box.

> train to be revise for develop working on

1 I hate _____ projects in groups, I prefer to work alone.
2 I never _____ exams, it's a waste of time.
3 I'd like to _____ a doctor or lawyer – they are the best jobs.
4 The best way to _____ your speaking skills is to go to an English-speaking country.

Are the statements true for you? In pairs, compare your answers.

Listening

3 Listen to the radio announcement about Trevor Baylis, a famous inventor, and answer the following question.

Which of the three radios below did Trevor Baylis invent?

4 Listen again and answer the following questions.

1 What makes Trevor like a typical inventor?
2 Why did he invent the wind-up radio?
3 What else has he invented?
4 What is he working on and developing at the moment?
5 What time does the programme start?

Grammar focus

5 Look at the examples in the box, then complete the sentences.

> A Trevor Baylis *has invented* a wind-up radio – it works very well.
> B He*'s been working* on a power device which creates electricity.

1 <u>Example A</u> is the *present perfect simple*.
2 _____ is the *present perfect continuous*.
3 _____ focuses on the results of past achievements.
4 _____ focuses on past, recent or current activities.
5 When we form the *present perfect simple*, we use *have/has* +
_____ .
6 When we form the *present perfect continuous*, we use *have/has* +
_____ + _____ .

Practice

6 <u>Underline</u> the correct verb forms in the sentences.

Example: <u>*She's won*</u> / *She's been winning* three prizes for dancing.

1 *I haven't revised* / *I haven't been revising* for my exam tomorrow, and now it's too late.
2 *Mick's received* / *Mick's been receiving* a gold certificate for lifesaving.
3 *I've worked on* / *I've been working on* my typing skills, but I still make mistakes!
4 They're exhausted because *they've trained* / *they've been training* for next week's marathon.
5 *I've passed* / *I've been passing* all my exams and now I'm going on holiday!
6 At last, *I've finished* / *I've been finishing* working on that project.
7 *He's tried* / *He's been trying* to get a new job but *he hasn't had* / *he hasn't been having* a single interview so far.

7 🔊 Listen to the sentences and check your answers to Exercise 6. Repeat the sentences with the correct pronunciation.

Get talking ...

8 Discuss your achievements and current projects.

1 Write three sentences about things you have *achieved* in your life.

Example: *I've passed all my English exams.*

2 Write three sentences about things you've been *working on / doing*.

Example: *I've been having judo lessons.*

3 In groups, compare and discuss your achievements and projects.

... and writing

9 Write part of the application letter for one of the following things describing your achievements and any projects in progress.

- A job you would like to have.
- A club you would like to join.

Language to go

A: What have you been doing recently?
B: I've been revising for my exam.

> GRAMMAR REFERENCE PAGE 114
> PRACTICE PAGE 101

Vocabulary Prison
Function Prohibition, obligation and permission in the past
Language to go Discussing freedom

Long walk to freedom

They only let me write one letter every six months. It was one of the facts of prison life. In prison, the only thing worse than bad news about one's family is no news at all. Mail was delivered once a month, and sometimes six months would go by without a letter. Often the authorities would keep mail out of spite. I can remember warders saying, 'Mandela, we have received a letter for you, but we cannot give it to you.' No explanation of why, or who the letter was from.

When letters did arrive, they were cherished. A letter was like the summer rain that could make even the desert bloom. When I was handed a letter by the authorities, I would not rush forward and grab it as I felt like doing, but take it slowly. Though I wanted to tear it open and read it, I would not give the authorities the satisfaction of seeing my eagerness, and I would return slowly to my cell as though I had many things to occupy me before opening a letter from my family.

Adapted from *Long Walk to Freedom* by Nelson Mandela

Vocabulary and speaking

1 **In pairs, describe the photos. Then discuss the following questions.**

1 Why was Nelson Mandela *arrested*?
2 Where was the *prison*? Was it *strict*?
3 What were the *cells* like?
4 What did the *warders* tell the *prisoners* to do?
5 Did the prisoners do any exercise?

2 ▭ **Listen to an extract from Nelson Mandela's book *Long Walk to Freedom* and check your answers.**

Reading

3 **In pairs, discuss the following question.**

What rules do you think the prison at Robben Island had about writing and receiving letters, and visits?

4 a) Work in groups.

Group A: Read the text on page 58.
Are the sentences true (T) or false (F)?

1 Mandela received letters regularly.
2 He could write letters as often as he wanted to.
3 He'd open the letters as soon as he received them.
4 He didn't want the prison officers to know how much they meant to him.

Group B: Turn to page 85.
Read your text and answer your questions.

b) Tell a partner from the other group about the rules.

Language focus

5 Read the examples in the box showing past obligation, permission and prohibition.

> A He *had to break* stones.
> B They *made him work* in silence.
> C They *let him write* a letter every six months.
> D He *was allowed to have* visits of 30 minutes.

Rewrite examples A–D in the negative.

6 a) Complete the rules using the correct form of the words in *italics* from Exercise 5.

1 It was necessary (past obligation)
  <u>had to</u> or <u>made</u>.
2 It wasn't necessary (no past obligation)
  _____ or _____ .
3 It was OK to do something (past permission)
  _____ or _____ .
4 It wasn't OK to do something (past prohibition)
  _____ or _____ .

b) Complete the sentences.

1 *Made* and *let* are followed by _____ + infinitive.
2 *Was / were allowed to* and *had to* are followed by _____ .

Practice

7 Complete the sentences using the verbs in brackets and the correct form of *made, let, had to* or *allowed to*. There may be more than one answer.

Example: They <u>made him stay</u> in a very small cell. (stay)

1 Mandela's prison warders only _____ for 30 minutes a day. (exercise)
2 In the past, many prisoners _____ chains. (wear)
3 Our family was very relaxed about rules, and I _____ home any time I wanted. (come)
4 My grandmother was very strict – she _____ at the dinner table at her house. (talk)
5 My parents gave me no choice. I _____ my room tidy. (keep)
6 There was a 'no smoking' rule at my school. The teachers and the students _____ anywhere. (smoke)
7 Some warders were kind. They _____ when I was ill. (work).

8 🔊 Listen to the sentences and check your answers to Exercise 7. Repeat the sentences with the correct pronunciation.

Get talking

9 Look at the words below and think about the times in your life when you had most or least freedom.

- family life
- university
- marriage
- a holiday
- school
- a job
- military service
- a political system

In groups, compare and discuss your ideas on freedom.

Language to go

A: What rules did you have at school, Dad?
B: Well, the main one was we weren't allowed to enjoy ourselves.

> GRAMMAR REFERENCE PAGE 114
> PRACTICE PAGE 101

Vocabulary   Doing business
Grammar   First and second conditionals
Language to go   Talking about likely and unlikely situations

Shaking hands

Speaking and vocabulary

1   **In pairs, discuss the following questions.**

1   What kind of meetings do you go to?
2   What do you like / dislike about meetings?
3   'Meetings are not work, they are *about* work.'
    Do you agree?
4   Are there any 'rules' you should follow in meetings?

2   **Complete the text with the verbs in the box in the correct tense.**

offer   exchange   make (x2)   negotiate   do   go

'I **went** on an important business trip for my company last month. My boss decided he wanted to ¹ _____ business with a new Internet company, so I ² _____ contact with their Marketing Manager. They were interested in talking to us too, and we ³ _____ an appointment to meet the following week. I was going to take a present for him, but then I decided not to. He might think I was ⁴ _____ him a bribe, to persuade him unfairly. When we met, we shook hands and ⁵ _____ business cards. The meeting was friendly, and we managed to ⁶ _____ a deal that both companies were happy with.'

Reading and listening

3 In pairs, do the quiz about business customs around the world.

How do you do business around the world?

Try this quick quiz to test your business knowledge

	T	F
1 It's common to be offered coffee or mint tea in offices in the Middle East.	☐	☐
2 People rush business in the Middle East.	☐	☐
3 In a pub in the UK, you should always buy some drinks for your group.	☐	☐
4 Business lunches in the US go on for a long time.	☐	☐
5 You should make sure you're not late for a meeting in the US.	☐	☐
6 Business people in the US will probably use first names from the beginning.	☐	☐
7 In the US, a business person will probably think a present is a bribe.	☐	☐
8 In Thailand, a business person will open a present immediately.	☐	☐

4 🔲 Listen and check your answers to Exercise 3.

5 Listen again and correct the statements that are false.

Grammar focus

6 Look at the examples in the box and complete the following rules.

> A *If you **have** a business lunch, it'**ll** probably only **last** an hour.*
> B *If you **gave** them a present, they **would** probably **think** it was a bribe.*

1 Example A is the _____ conditional: *If +* _____ , _____ .
2 Example B is the _____ conditional: *If +* _____ , _____ .
3 In example A, the speaker thinks this is *likely / unlikely* to happen.
4 In example B, the speaker thinks this is *likely / unlikely* to happen.

7 Look at the recording script for Exercise 4 on page 122 and find other examples of the first and second conditional.

Practice

8 **Decide how likely each situation below is for you.**

Example: A friend invites you for a coffee after the class. Likely
A friend invites you out to dinner after the class. Unlikely

1 A friend asks you to give his nephew a job.
2 You decide to get a new job this year.
3 You're an hour late for an important business meeting.
4 You're still in a meeting two hours after your finishing time.
5 It's sunny tomorrow.
6 A business partner offers you a bribe.
7 Your boss asks you to move to another country for your job.
8 One of your employees makes a lot of private phone calls.

9 **Now write sentences saying what you *will* or *would do* in each situation.**

Example: If a friend invites me for a coffee after the class, I'll say yes.

If a friend invited me out to dinner after the class, I'd be surprised, but I'd say yes!

Get talking

10 In groups, discuss your ideas from Exercises 8 and 9.

What will you do if ...?
What would you do if ...?

Language to go

> A: What would you do if someone offered you a bribe?
> B: I'd ask what they wanted and see if the bribe was enough!

> GRAMMAR REFERENCE PAGE 114
> PRACTICE PAGE 102

Vocabulary   The weather
Grammar   Reported statements
Language to go Reporting what you hear or read

Sunshine and showers

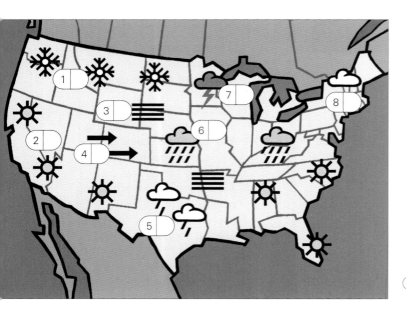

Vocabulary and speaking

1 **Look at the weather map and match the words in the box with the symbols on the map.**

> a) cloud   b) fog   c) rain   d) showers   e) snow
> f) sunshine   g) thunderstorms   h) wind

2 **Complete the following sentences using the words in the box.**

> heavy (x2)   thick (x2)   severe
> strong   bright   light

1 There was _____ rain during the night and some roads were flooded.
2 You won't really need an umbrella – there will just be _____ showers.
3 A tree was hit by lightning during _____ thunderstorms yesterday.
4 It isn't raining today, but there's very _____ cloud.
5 _____ snow will fall tonight, especially in the mountains.
6 There was a very _____ wind and several trees were blown down.
7 It was difficult to see while I was driving because of the _____ fog.
8 During the summer in Greece, there is _____ sunshine every day.

3 **In pairs, discuss the following questions.**

1 What is the weather like today?
2 What weather is typical of different parts of your country?
3 What type of weather do you prefer? Why?
4 Has the weather ever ruined a special occasion for you?
5 Are there any sayings about the weather in your country?

Listening

4 **Match the pictures with the correct statement.**

1 My friend has psychic powers – he uses his dreams to predict the weather.

2 My grandmother predicts the weather using signs from nature.

3 I usually believe the weather reports on the TV and radio.

Steve and Danuta invite

_____

to celebrate their wedding on
Saturday 21st July
at St Mark's Church
at 3 p.m.
Reception to be held at Harwood House
and Gardens (weather permitting)

5 In pairs, discuss what you think the people in each picture in Exercise 4 will say about the weather tomorrow for Steve and Danuta's wedding. Write your ideas in column 1 below.

	What do you think they will say?	What weather do they predict?
Danuta's grandmother		
Steve's friend		
The weather reporter on TV		

Now listen and check your answers. Complete column 2.

6 Listen to people speaking after the wedding. Whose prediction was the most accurate?

Grammar focus

7 Look at the examples of reported speech in the box. Then look at the recording script for Exercise 5 on page 122 and answer the following question.

> A *I told them* the sky *had been* very red *that morning.*
> B *They said* that there *would be* rain and winds *in the following 24 hours.*

What did they actually say? Find the direct speech for examples A and B above.

8 **a) Complete the rules with *said* or *told*.**

You can start reported speech with:
1 Subject (*I, you* etc.) + _____ + Object (me, them etc.)
2 Subject (*I, you* etc.) + _____

b) Underline the correct alternative.

After *said* or *told*, you *need / don't need* that.

9 Look at the recording script for Exercise 6 on page 122 and find examples of reported speech. Then underline the correct alternatives below.

When changing from direct speech to reported speech:
1 the tenses usually *move one back / stay the same.*
2 the time expressions usually *change / don't change.*

Practice

10 Rewrite the sentences in reported speech. Make any necessary changes.

Example: It'll rain for most of the day. (She said…)
She said it would rain for most of that day.

1 I feel sure about this. (She told us…)
2 You'll just have to have the party inside. (She told them…)
3 Dreams can tell us a lot. (He said…)
4 I've been dreaming about blue. (He told us…)
5 I was lying on a tropical beach last night. (He said…)
6 I'm never wrong. (He told them…)
7 The weather for tomorrow is looking very changeable. (She said…)
8 Thunderstorms will be everywhere by the morning. (She told us…)
9 We'll be back after the late news. (She said…)

Get talking

11 **Report what people say.**

1 Work in groups.

Group A: Turn to page 85.
Group B: Turn to page 86.
Group C: Turn to page 87.
Prepare to report your information about tomorrow's weather.

2 Make new groups. Using all the information, decide together what the weather will be like tomorrow. Are you going to have the garden party that you planned?

3 Check the actual weather on the day of the party on page 87. Were you correct?

Language to go

A: Have you heard the weather report?
B: Yes. They said there would be heavy rain all day.

> GRAMMAR REFERENCE PAGE 114
> PRACTICE PAGE 102

LESSON **31**

The past

Vocabulary   Things we read
Grammar   Past perfect simple and continuous
Language to go   Talking about important moments

Turning points

Vocabulary and speaking

1 **Match the quotations with the words in the box.**

> a) a best-seller   b) magazines
> c) a newspaper   d) a textbook
> e) a novel   f) a play
> g) poetry   h) websites

2 **In pairs, discuss the following questions.**

1 Have you read a good book recently?
2 What type of thing do you read most?
3 When do you usually read?
4 What did you read, or what was read to you, when you were a child?

Reading

3 **In pairs, discuss this question.**

What do you know about J K Rowling and her books?

4 **Read the article and explain the title.**

5 **Read the article again and put these events in the order they happened.**

Example: 1 f   2 ...

a) worked as an English teacher
b) moved to Portugal
c) worked as a French teacher
d) studied French at university
e) moved to Edinburgh
f) wrote a story called *Rabbit*
g) became a best-seller writer
h) first novel was published
i) returned to the UK

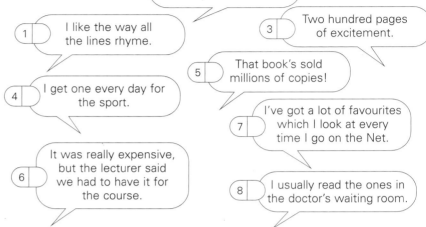

1   I like the way all the lines rhyme.

2   I saw it at the *Royal Theatre*.

3   Two hundred pages of excitement.

4   I get one every day for the sport.

5   That book's sold millions of copies!

6   It was really expensive, but the lecturer said we had to have it for the course.

7   I've got a lot of favourites which I look at every time I go on the Net.

8   I usually read the ones in the doctor's waiting room.

A suitcase o

J K Rowling (the J is for Joanne) is a best-selling author. Her books are written for children, but adults love them too. In 1996, her big moment came when she heard that her first novel, *Harry Potter and the Philosopher's Stone*, would be published. 'The moment I found out was one of the best of my life,' says Joanne.

Before 1996, Joanne had been living in Portugal and teaching English. When she returned to the UK, she had a suitcase of fantastic stories about Harry Potter. She moved to Edinburgh and became a French teacher. It was there that she decided to finish the *Harry* novel and get it published.

As a child, Joanne had always loved writing and before she was six, she had finished her first story about a rabbit called *Rabbit*. From then on she followed her love of language. She enjoyed English at school and went on to study French at university.

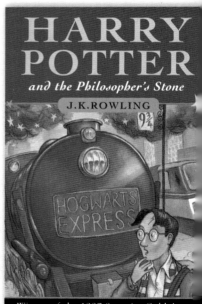

Having achieved her ambition, what does she say about writing? 'Writing can be a lot of fun. It can also be a lot of hard work, but don't let that put you off! My advice young writers is to read as much as you can, like I did. It will give you understanding of what makes good writing and it will enlarge yo vocabulary. Start by writing about things you know about – your ov experiences and feelings. That's what I do.'

Grammar focus

6 **Look at the examples then complete the rules. Write** *activity* **or** *action*.

> A **Past perfect simple**
> Before she was six, she **had finished** her first story.
> B **Past perfect continuous**
> Before 1996, she **had been living** in Portugal.
>
> | She finished | She had been |
> | her first story | living in Portugal |
>
> She was six   1996   now

1 We use the *past perfect simple* to talk about an _____ that happened at a time before another time in the past.
2 We use the *past perfect continuous* to talk about an _____ that happened at a time before another time in the past.

tories

Practice

7 **Rewrite the sentences putting the verbs in brackets in the correct tenses.**

Example: She (work) there for ten years before she (become) the director.
She had been working there for ten years before she became the director.

1 He (score) a goal after they (play) for nearly ninety minutes.
2 He (pass) the exam because he (study) so hard.
3 They (go out) together for two years when they (decide) to get married.
4 I finally (win) a big prize after I (buy) lottery tickets all my life.
5 They (hope for) a baby girl but in the end they (have) a boy.
6 She (plan) her retirement for a long time before she (be) sixty.
7 I (understand) the past perfect continuous after I (study) it for three weeks.

Get talking

8 **Talk about important moments in your life.**

1 Think about an important moment in your life. It could be about one of the following things:
   - work
   - relationships
   - family
   - friends
   - travel
   - studies

2 Make notes about the important moment and the background events. (What had been happening before then?)

3 In groups, tell your stories.

Language to go

> A: Why did you change jobs?
> B: I'd been working there for ten years and I was bored.

> GRAMMAR REFERENCE PAGE 115
> PRACTICE PAGE 103

Vocabulary Housework and cleanliness
Grammar *Have something done* and reflexive pronouns
Language to go Things you do, and have done for you

Clean and tidy

Vocabulary and speaking

1 <u>Underline</u> the correct alternatives in the sentences.

1 *Homework / Housework* is very important: you should always have a *tidy / messy* house.
2 It's a woman's job to *wash / vacuum* the clothes and *do / make* the ironing.

3 Most teenagers have *tidy / messy* bedrooms, with CDs and clothes all over the floor.

4 The person who cooked should *make / do* the dishes afterwards.
5 It's a man's job to *do / make* the gardening and *do / wash* the car.

2 In pairs, discuss the sentences in Exercise 1. Do you agree?

Reading

3 Look at the beginning of the advertisement for Maid4U and discuss the following question.

What kind of services do you think they offer?

Now read the rest of the advertisement and check your ideas.

4 Match the headlines with the correct paragraph in the advertisement.

School's out

Shopping special

Treat yourself

Home services

Maid4U

Services for your home

At **Maid4U** we understand that you can't do everything yourself. You have a busy life, you work hard and you'd like to have all the boring things done by somebody else. Sounds familiar? Then read on...

1 [   ]

No time to do the housework when you get home? Have all your washing and ironing done – **Maid4U**'s service is quick and efficient and it doesn't cost much.

'After our daughter's 21st birthday party, the house was a complete mess, but luckily I had it cleaned from top to bottom with **Maid4U**'s special "After Party" service.'
Sue Lloyd, Birmingham.

Grammar focus

> A You can't do everything *yourself*.
> B *Have* all your *washing and ironing done*.

5 **a) Look at example A and <u>underline</u> the correct alternatives.**

We use reflexive pronouns when:
1 the subject and the object are *the same / different.*
2 we want to make the subject *stronger / weaker.*

b) Write the reflexive pronouns to complete the list.

me	_____	it	_____
you	*yourself*	we	_____
him	_____	you	_____
her	_____	they	_____

...ke cooking but can't stand going to the supermarket? Have all your weekly shopping done with our latest service. We'll even write your shopping list and suggest menus for you.
*'I've been using **Maid4U** for years now – it means I don't have to think about what to cook at the end of a long day.'*
Mrs Wells, London.

...ave you ever had your hair cut in the comfort of ...our own home? Michelle Baker has ...
...With three young children, ...never had time to treat ...nyself and go to the ...airdresser's or beauty ...alon. Now I don't have ...! I've been having my ...air and nails done at ...ome for over a year now – ... look, and feel, great!'
...1. Baker, Chester.

Too busy to pick the children up from school yourself? Tell us where and when – and we'll do it for you. Our fully qualified staff will even stay and read your kids a bedtime story.

All **YOU** have to do is phone us – **WE** will do the rest for you!
☎ **01799 323323**

6 **a) Look at example B and answer the question.**

What does *have + something + past participle* mean? Do you:
1 do something yourself?
2 ask (and usually pay) *someone else* to do something?

b) <u>Underline</u> examples of *have + something + past participle* in the text. What tenses are used?

Practice

7 **Complete the dialogues. Use the correct form of *have + something + past participle* and reflexive pronouns.**

Example: A: Would you ever **have your feet massaged**? (feet / massage)
B: No, I'd rather **do it myself**. (do / it)

1 A: Your hair looks nice! _____ (cut / it) at *The Hair Salon*?
   B: No, I _____ . (cut / it)
2 A: My car is very dirty, but I don't want to _____ . (clean / it)
   B: Why don't you _____ (clean / it) at that new Valet Service?
3 A: Mick and Daniela are organising a big party.
   B: Are they _____ (organise / it all)?
   A: Yes. They don't like _____ (organise / things) by other people.
4 A: My bicycle is broken. I usually _____ (repair / it) but I haven't got time.
   B: I _____ (repair / mine) at *The Bike Shop* last week.

Get talking

8 **Look at the advertisement again and discuss the following questions.**

1 What other services do you think they might offer?
   Example: *dog-walking services*
2 From the list of services:
   • What do you do yourself?
   • What do you have done?
   • If you were very rich, what would you have done?
   • What do you think you should only do yourself?

> GRAMMAR REFERENCE PAGE 115
> PRACTICE PAGE 103

Vocabulary   Describing changes
Grammar   Future with *will* and *will have done*
Language to go   Predicting future events

Tomorrow's world

Vocabulary and speaking

1   **Look at the verbs in the box and divide them into two groups under the correct headings.**

> go up / go down   decrease / increase   fall / rise
> improve / deteriorate   climb / drop
> get better / get worse

good / bad changes	up / down changes
	go up / go down

2   **In pairs, discuss what changes you think will happen in the future to do with ...**

- pollution
- crime
- the birthrate in your country
- employment in your country
- your salary
- life expectancy
- the number of car users

Example: **I think pollution will start to decrease.**

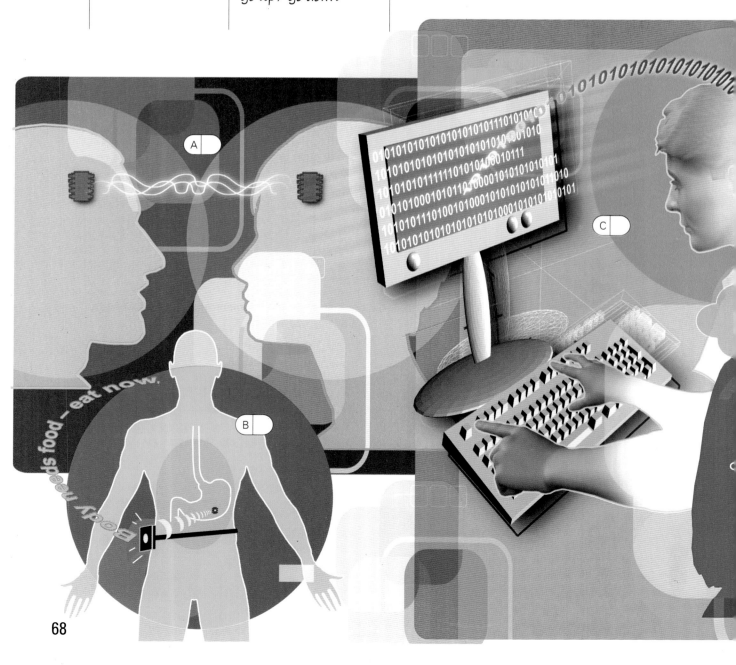

Listening

3 In pairs, look at the pictures of future inventions and describe what you think is happening.

4  Listen to four experts talking about these inventions. Write the number of each speaker next to the correct picture.

5 Listen again and write down the year by which each speaker predicts the inventions could be available.

Prediction	Year
1 'Brainlink' computer 2 More robots than people 3 Edible computers 4 Communication by brainwaves	

Grammar focus

6 Look at the examples in the box. Then look at the recording script for Exercise 4 on page 122 and find other examples of these future forms.

> A *will + have +* past participle:
>   ... scientists **will have perfected** the 'brainlink' computer.
>
> B *will +* infinitive:
>   ... you **will be** able to download information into your head.

7 <u>Underline</u> the correct alternatives.

1 We use *will + have +* past participle when we expect something to happen *before/at/after* a point in future time.
2 We use *will +* infinitive when we expect something to happen *before/at/after* a point in future time.

Cześć!

Practice

8 **Find the mistake in each sentence and correct it.**

Example: Life expectancy will have ~~increase~~ to over a hundred by 2070. ✗ *increased*

1 Can I give you this tomorrow? I won't finished it by 5.00 today.
2 In the next five years, communication will have became much quicker.
3 I'll probably have reached the airport for 3.30.
4 By 2035, they will have building underground cities in Japan.
5 They have developed totally automated factories by 2025.
6 Don't call him at 7.30, he'll has gone out by then.
7 They will have been designed robots for guiding blind people by 2020.

Get talking

9 **In pairs, make predictions about your own and each other's lives.**

1 Think about education, jobs, family, sports and hobbies, travel etc.

	Me	My partner
By 2010		
By 2015		
By 2020	*got married*	
By 2025		

2 In pairs, discuss your predictions.

Do you think your partner's predictions about you will come true?

> ### Language to go
>
> A: When will you finish your homework?
> B: I'll probably have finished it by about 2015!

> GRAMMAR REFERENCE PAGE 115
> PRACTICE PAGE 104

LESSON **34**
Vocabulary

Vocabulary 1   Medical problems and symptoms
Vocabulary 2   Phrasal verbs about illness
Language to go   Describing symptoms of an illness

Honeymoon horrors

Vocabulary and speaking

1   **a) Complete the sentences with the verbs in the box.**

> ache   itch   bite   cut   sting   swell up

1   Don't touch that bee – it might _____ you.
2   If your feet _____ any more, you won't be able to put your shoes on.
3   It was a big dog with sharp teeth – I thought it was going to _____ me.
4   I've been standing up all day and my legs really _____ now.
5   My hands _____ when I wear gloves made of wool.
6   Be careful not to _____ yourself with that knife – it's really sharp.

b) Complete the table.

Verbs	Nouns	Adjectives or participles
ache	*an ache*	*achy*
bite		
cut		
itch		
sting		
swell up		

2   **In pairs, discuss the following questions.**

1   When you go on holiday, what things do you take as precautions against accidents and illness?
2   Have you ever fallen ill when you were in a foreign country? If so, what happened?

Listening

3   **In pairs, look at the four pictures below and predict what happened to the people on their honeymoons.**

4   **▭▭ Listen and check your predictions and match the speaker with the correct picture.**

Speaker	Picture	Country	What happened?	Symptoms
1				
2				
3				
4				

Now listen again and complete the table.

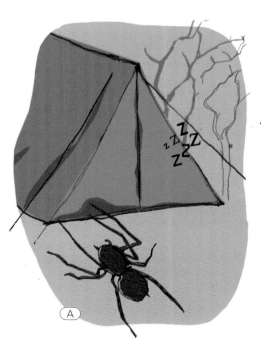
(A)

(B)

(C)

Vocabulary focus

5 **a) Look at the phrasal verbs in the box, then turn to the recording script on pages 122–3 and find one example for each.**

> a) swell up   b) pass out   c) come out in
> d) turn into   e) come down with
> f) throw up   g) get over

b) Match the phrasal verbs in the box with the correct definitions.

1 become
2 catch (an illness)
3 get bigger
4 lose consciousness
5 return to a normal state of health
6 suddenly become covered (in spots)
7 vomit *(informal)*

6 **Divide the phrasal verbs in Exercise 5 into two groups under the correct headings.**

Transitive (an object is necessary)	Intransitive (an object is not necessary)
turn into (something)	

7 🎧 **Listen to the sentences and mark the stress on the phrasal verbs.**

Example: I thought I was going to pass out. ☐

What is the general rule about stress in phrasal verbs?

Practice

8 **Rewrite the sentences using the appropriate phrasal verbs.**

Example: The room was so hot she lost consciousness.
The room was so hot she passed out.

1 Last year, I caught a dangerous illness just before my exams.
2 I hurt my foot – it got very big and I couldn't put my shoe on.
3 My brother had food poisoning last week – he vomited all night.
4 You must go to the doctor – an infection can suddenly become something very bad.
5 I'm allergic to fish – I become covered in red spots if I eat it.
6 She'll be back at work when she's returned to her normal state of health after the flu.

Get talking

9 **Describe symptoms and give advice.**

1 Work in pairs to roleplay a visit to the doctor.

Student A: Turn to page 86 and find out your symptoms.
Student B: Turn to page 87 and find out the advice you give to Student A.

2 Change roles. Student B is now the patient and Student A is the doctor.

Language to go

A: What's the matter?
B: My fingers are swollen and I've come out in red spots.

> GRAMMAR REFERENCE PAGE 116
> PRACTICE PAGE 104

Vocabulary   People and groups
Grammar   Past modal verbs of deduction
Language to go   Drawing conclusions about the past

Ice maiden

Vocabulary

1   Match the words in the box with the definitions below.

> culture   family   generation
> society   status   team

1   _____ – grandparents, parents, brothers etc.
2   _____ – a group of people who work or play together
3   _____ – the beliefs and art made by a group of people
4   _____ – all members of a family of about the same age
5   _____ – people living together with the same laws etc.
6   _____ – social or professional position (in relation to other people)

Speaking and reading

2   Look at the pictures below. In pairs, discuss the following questions.

1   Who are these people? What are they doing?
2   What do you think they discovered?

3   Read the introduction to the article and check your answers.

4   Read these facts about the Ice Maiden and discuss possible reasons for them in pairs.

1   She was very tall.
2   She was dressed like a man.
3   She had a very big headdress.
4   She had a hole in her head.
5   She had tattoos of animals on her body.

5   Now read the rest of the article on the opposite page and check your ideas.

An amazing discovery

In 1993, an amazing discovery was made in the Siberian mountains. A team of archaeologists found a woman – she was 2,500 years old. They called her the Ice Maiden because the ice had preserved her body, her clothes and her possessions. They discovered that she was from the Pazyryk people who had once lived there. And by looking at her things, they realised that she must have been someone very special. But who was she? And what was her position in society?

Grammar focus

6 **a) Complete the example sentences from the article, then answer the question.**

> A She *might* …
> B She *could* …
> C She *can't* …
> D She *must* …

In examples A to D, are we talking about a situation in the past or in the present?

b) Match the example sentences with the correct meaning in the table below.

Sentence	Meaning of modal phrases
	It's certainly not true.
	It's possibly true.
	It's certainly true.
	It's possibly true.

One metre seventy The team found that the Ice Maiden was one metre seventy in height – extremely tall for a woman at that time. It is not clear why she was so tall – she might have had extra food because of her status.

Dressed like a man The Ice Maiden was dressed exactly like a man, which means that she could have worked as a soldier. And only important people wore tall headdresses – she was wearing a metre-tall headdress. It was covered in gold which clearly showed she was a rich and powerful woman.

Hole in the head The archaeologists found a large hole in the back of her head. This was probably part of a process for preserving important people when they died. This young woman clearly can't have been an ordinary member of society.

Fabulous tattoos Her body was covered with fabulous tattoos. The archaeologists now think that she must have been a storyteller. Storytellers were very important members of the Pazyryk society. They memorised the history of their people and used the tattoos of animals to illustrate the stories. In this way, they passed on the beliefs and traditions to future generations.

Practice

7 **Write sentences using the information given below to draw conclusions about the past. There may be more than one answer.**

Example: gold headdress … She / rich
She must have been rich.

1 very tall … She / special medical care
2 remembered long stories …. She / good memory
3 car broke down … He / run out of petrol
4 woke up late … He / not hear his alarm clock
5 no answer at the door … He / go out
6 very late for dinner … They / get lost
7 my bicycle is missing … Someone / borrow it
8 fail the exam … She / not study much

Get talking …

8 **Draw conclusions about the past.**

1 Make notes about what you think life was like 2,500 years ago. These ideas may help you.

- entertainment
- families
- farming
- houses
- illness
- religion
- culture
- transport
- food

2 In groups, discuss your ideas and explain your reasons.

… and writing

9 **Write a paragraph using the notes you made in Exercise 8 and the ideas you talked about. Compare life in the past with your life today.**

Language to go

A: Life must have been harder 1,000 years ago.
B: Yes, but it might have been quieter.

> GRAMMAR REFERENCE PAGE 116
> PRACTICE PAGE 105

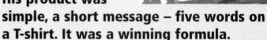

	Vocabulary	Business processes: word building
	Grammar	Non-defining relative clauses
	Language to go	Giving extra information

A winning formula

Vocabulary and speaking

1 Complete the sentences with the appropriate form of the nouns or verbs in the box.

Specific noun	General noun	Verb
(a) product	production	(to) produce
(a) market	marketing	(to) market
(a) business plan	planning	(to) plan
(a) business	business	(to) do business
(an) advert	advertising	(to) advertise

1 Traditionally, the two main _____ from Brazil were coffee and gold.
2 _____ is very good at the moment – we're making a lot of money.
3 The _____ department deals with _____ and publicity.
4 They did a lot of _____ before they built the new supermarket.
5 You have to show the bank a _____ before they'll lend you the money.
6 Our company doesn't *make* clothes but we _____ clothes made by other companies.
7 Have you seen that funny toothpaste _____ on TV?

2 In pairs, discuss the statements below. Do you agree?

> The best ideas are never planned.

> If you advertise something enough, people will buy it.

> The most successful products are the simplest ones.

Reading

3 Read the first paragraph of the text to find out what Toby Mott's 'winning formula' was.

4 Read the whole text. What do the following numbers refer to?

5 20 36 40 60,000

5 Read the text again and answer the following questions.

1 Why did he decide to start his own business?
2 Where does he find new phrases?
3 What do his friends think about him?

A simple idea

Toby Mott was just an ordinary person who worked as an artist. But then, at the age of 36, he had an idea which made him famous. It started when he wanted to earn some money for Christmas one year. His product was simple, a short message – five words on a T-shirt. It was a winning formula.

He took the T-shirts to a clothes shop and they sold 40 in a week. Immediately, he decided to start his own business. The product was good, he got the business plan right and it worked. In the last twelve months, he has sold 60,000 T-shirts worldwide.

The phrases for the T-shirts come from things he thinks of during the day and from conversations with friends at dinner. His customers, who include the rich and the famous, enjoy his imaginative phrases. They include things like 'I will spend your money', 'I do things I shouldn't' and 'I have nothing to wear', which he sold to the top international model, Kate Moss.

Mott says, 'I'm successful, but it hasn't changed my personal life. I still work at home on the same small desk, where I produce all the designs. My friends, who I've known for more than twenty years, are still my friends.

'In fact, they're as surprised about my success as I am.'

Grammar focus

6 Look at the example of a non-defining relative clause in the box and answer the questions below.

> My friends, *who I've known for more than twenty years,* are still my friends.

1 Does the clause add extra or essential information about the 'friends'?
2 What relative pronoun is used to introduce this clause?
3 Will the sentence still make sense if the non-defining relative clause is removed?
4 What punctuation surrounds the non-defining relative clause?

7 Find three more examples in the text. What relative pronouns are used?

Adapted from *The Sunday Times*

Practice

8 Combine these sentences to make one sentence. Use a non-defining relative clause to give the extra information.

Example: My car needs a new engine. I have had it for ten years.
My car, which I have had for ten years, needs a new engine.

1 Her home town is in the north of the island. It has a population of 50,000.
2 Budapest has a large river. I went there on business last year.
3 His wife cooks wonderful Chinese food. She is from Hong Kong.
4 My football team keeps on losing! I have supported them for years.
5 That woman has opened her own shop. She is only 25.
6 My friend has decided to move to South Africa. His parents live in Cape Town.
7 That programme 'Entrepreneurs' is really good. It's on at 8 p.m.

Get talking ...

9 Explain a business plan.

1 You want to start a new business. In pairs, decide on a product.
2 Make a business plan to borrow money from the bank. Use the form below.
3 Explain your plan to another group.

> Product:
>
> Price:
>
> Publicity:
>
> Place:

... and writing

10 Write a letter to your bank manager. Give an outline of your idea, mention your plan and ask for help with the finance.

Language to go

A: Do you have a business plan?
B: Yes, I have a plan, which I wrote myself, and the perfect product.
A: Really? Tell me more.

> GRAMMAR REFERENCE PAGE 116
> PRACTICE PAGE 105

Vocabulary   Verb expressions about friendship
Grammar   Present perfect with *for* and *since*
Language to go   Describing friendship

Old friends

Vocabulary and speaking

1   Complete the sentences with the appropriate expressions in the box.

> am in touch with   keep in touch with   keep up with
> lost contact with   rely on   remain   send

1   I _____ cards to all my friends on their birthdays.

2   I _____ an old friend when he moved house and I lost his address.
3   I make hundreds of phone calls every week because it's important to _____ people.
4   If you have a problem, the only person you can really _____ is yourself.
5   I like to _____ all my friends' news and to know what's happening.
6   I had an argument with him. But I hope we can still _____ friends.
7   I _____ a lot of friends from my childhood – we write to each other regularly.

2   In pairs, discuss the sentences in Exercise 1 which are true for you.

3   In pairs, describe the men in the photo.

Do you think they are friends?

Listening

4   [image: cassette] Listen to James and Richard talking about their friendship and answer the questions. Do they say the same thing?

	James	Richard
1 How long have they been friends?		
2 Where did they first meet?		
3 Have they seen each other regularly over the years?		
4 How often do they see each other now?		
5 What do they do together?		

5   Listen again. Are there any other differences?

Grammar focus

6 Look at the examples below and <u>underline</u> the correct alternatives.

> A I**'ve known** him **for** 50 years.
>
> 50 years ago ————————————————|············· now
>
> B I**'ve been living** in Brighton **since** '99.
>
> ————————————————|·············
> 1999   now

1 A and B are talking about *actions or states which started in the past and continued until now / finished actions or states.*
2 We can't use the *present perfect continuous / present perfect simple* with stative verbs (e.g. know, like, believe).
3 We use *for / since* to refer to the start of the action.
4 We use *for / since* to refer to the period of time of the action.

Practice

7 Find the mistake in each sentence and correct it.

Example: I've been playing tennis ~~since~~ two hours. ✗ *for*

1 We have been knowing them for more than twenty years.
2 She's been won the competition for the last five years.
3 Had you visited your grandmother since her accident?
4 They haven't phone me for ages.
5 I'm doing my homework for two hours.
6 I've been liking her for a long time.
7 How long you have been living here?

8 🔢 Listen to the sentences and check your answers to Exercise 7. Repeat the sentences with the correct pronunciation.

Get talking

9 Talk about someone you have known for a long time.

In pairs, tell each other about a good friend. Use the questions in Exercise 4 to help you.

> GRAMMAR REFERENCE PAGE 116
> PRACTICE PAGE 106

Don't worry, be happy

Speaking and vocabulary

1   Read these words from the song *Don't worry, be happy* by Bobby McFerrin. In pairs, discuss the questions.

> *In every life we have some trouble,*
> *But when you worry you make it double.*
> *Don't worry, be happy.*

1   Do you agree with the singer?
2   Do you worry too much?
3   What do you worry about?
4   What helps you to stop worrying?

2   Look at the sentences and put the expressions in *italics* in the correct column.

unhappy	happy	very happy
depressed		

1   He's *depressed* because he's just lost his job.
2   Don't talk to her yet – she's always *in a bad mood* in the mornings.
3   I'm *glad* I went to Dave's party; it was really good.
4   He's feeling *miserable* about the cold, wet weather today.
5   Are you *pleased* with your new car?
6   I'm *in a good mood* today because my boss gave me a pay rise.
7   We'd be *delighted* to come to your daughter's wedding.
8   My dad is going to pay for a holiday to Australia! I'm absolutely *thrilled*!
9   I'm quite *satisfied* with my life – but I'm having a bad day today!

3   Look at the graph.

People were recently asked what three factors were most important in determining their happiness. What do you think they said? Guess which category goes with which percentage.

Now turn to page 87 to see if you were correct.

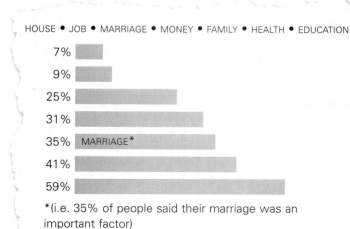

HOUSE • JOB • MARRIAGE • MONEY • FAMILY • HEALTH • EDUCATION

7%
9%
25%
31%
35%   MARRIAGE*
41%
59%

*(i.e. 35% of people said their marriage was an important factor)

Language focus

6 Look at the recording script for Exercise 4 on page 123 and complete the indirect questions in the box.

> A *Would you mind* _____ if you've ever seen ... ?
> B *Could you* _____ which you worry about more?
> C *Can I* _____ how you feel about ... ?
> D *I'd like* _____ how you feel about your job.

Now write the direct question for each one.

7 a) Complete the rules.

1 *Wh-* questions: _____ + subject + (modal verb) + _____
2 *Yes / No* questions: _____ + subject + (modal verb) + _____

b) Look at the recording script again and complete the sentence.

If you don't want to answer a question, you can say:

I'd _____ *not to answer that one* or *I'd* _____ *not say.*

Practice

8 Write indirect questions. Use the words in brackets to start.

Example: How do you feel about birthdays? (Could you ... ?)
Could you tell me how you feel about birthdays?

1 Are you generally an optimistic person? (I'd like ...)
2 Are you happy with your job? (Can I ... ?)
3 Did you wake up in a good mood this morning? (Could you ... ?)
4 How would you react if someone damaged your car? (I'd like ...)
5 How would you feel about winning the lottery? (Would you ... ?)
6 Do you worry about getting old? (Could you ... ?)
7 Do you like answering personal questions? (Can I ... ?)

9 [cassette] Listen and repeat the questions in Exercise 8.

Listening

4 [cassette] Listen to a man answering questions in a survey in the street. Which topics from Exercise 3 do they talk about?

5 Listen again. Are these sentences true (T) or false (F)?

1 The man is happy to take part in the survey.
2 He refuses to answer some of the questions.
3 He has an unhappy marriage.
4 He likes being on time.

Get talking ...

10 In pairs, ask and answer the questions in Exercise 8.

11 [cassette] Listen to the song and read the words on page 86.

Language to go

A: Could you tell me if you like answering personal questions?
B: I'd rather not say.

> GRAMMAR REFERENCE PAGE 116
> PRACTICE PAGE 106

LESSON **39**
Conditionals

Vocabulary   Shopping
Grammar   Third conditional and *I wish / If only*
Language to go   Talking about past regrets

If only...

Vocabulary and speaking

1 Complete the sentences using the words or
expressions in the box.

> the sales   buy things on impulse   get a bargain
> haggling   refund   go window shopping
> shop around   take things back   try clothes on

1 Do you _____ and look at a lot of things
without intending to buy them?
2 Do you ever _____ without planning to?
3 Do you wait until _____ at the end of the
season, to _____ ?
4 Do you _____ in different places to
compare prices?
5 How often do you _____ to the shop and
ask for a _____ ?
6 How do you feel about _____ for a
cheaper price?
7 Do you always _____ to see if they fit
before buying them?

2 In pairs, ask and answer the
completed questions.

Reading

3 In pairs, discuss the following.

1 What kind of things do people
buy when they are on holiday?
2 Do you normally buy souvenirs?

4 Read the story about Dave and
Liz, two English tourists in India.
Are the sentences true (T) or
false (F)?

1 The hatseller said the hats cost
fifty rupees.
2 Dave felt he had paid too much.
3 Dave wanted to change his mind
about buying the hat.
4 Liz thought Dave had paid too
much.
5 Dave decided not to wear the
hat again.

You buy hat?

On our first full day in Delhi we went to the Red Fort.
A man just outside was selling floppy hats, wearing a
huge pile of them on his head.
 'Hello, friend. You buy hat?'
 'How much?'
 'Best price.'
 'How much?'
 'What you like.'
 'What I like?'
 'You give price.'
 'How much are they normally?'
 'You give price, friend. Any price – cheap price.'
 'Um … 50 rupees?'
 This seemed reasonable to me, but when I said it, he
immediately put a hat on my head and waited for me to
pay. I'd obviously offered too much, but I didn't really
see how I could change my mind, so I gave him the
cash.
 Liz asked me what I had paid and laughed in my
face. I said I didn't care, and thought it was a perfectly
fair price for what I had got, because it was a very cool
hat. 'Haven't you noticed that every other Westerner in
the city is wearing one?'
 I looked around to see if what she had said was true.
A group of middle-aged Europeans came out of the fort.
More than half of them were wearing my hat.
 I wish I hadn't bought the hat now, but thanks to the
argument I'd have to wear it all the time, just to show
that she hadn't changed my mind.

Adapted from *Are You Experienced?* by William Sutcliffe

Grammar focus

5 **Look at the examples in the box and answer the questions.**

> A *I wish* I hadn't bought the hat.
> B *If only* I hadn't bought the hat.
> C *If I hadn't bought* the hat, I *wouldn't have felt* so stupid.

1 Did he buy the hat?
2 How does he feel about it now?

6 **a) <u>Underline</u> the correct alternatives.**

1 In examples A and B
   I wish and *If only* are followed by the *past simple / past perfect simple*.

2 Example C is the third conditional. We use the third conditional to talk about how things *were / may have been different* in the past.

b) Complete the rules.

The form of the third conditional is:
If + _____ + _____ , *would* + _____ + _____ .

Practice

7 **Write two sentences for each question. First use *I wish* or *If only*, then the third conditional.**

Example: I bought that skirt on impulse. I wasted my money.
I wish / If only I hadn't bought that skirt on impulse.
If I hadn't bought that skirt on impulse, I wouldn't have wasted my money.

1 I went to bed late. I felt tired in the morning.
2 I didn't start my homework early enough. I didn't finish it.
3 I forgot my mother's birthday. She got upset.
4 I didn't pay attention at school. I failed my exam.
5 I arrived late for the interview. I didn't get the job.
6 I told my friend she looked fat. She never spoke to me again.

Get talking

8 **Is it true that 'you only regret what you don't do'?**

1 Think about one thing you regret …
   • doing • not doing • saying • not saying

2 In groups, discuss your regrets.

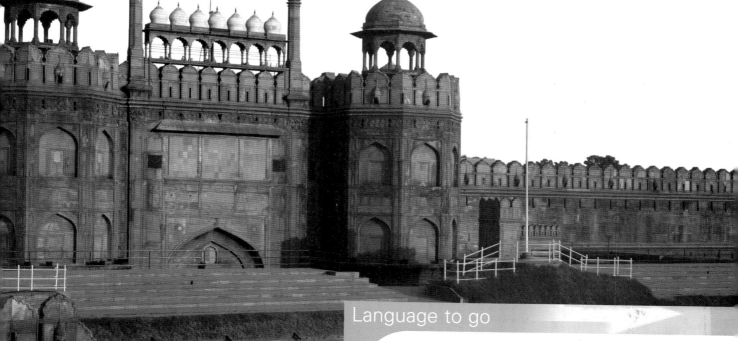

Language to go

A: Those jeans were expensive and they don't fit you.
B: I know. I wish I hadn't bought them.

LESSON **40**
Verb patterns

Vocabulary Job applications and interviews
Grammar Reported questions
Language to go Reporting a conversation or interview

How did it go?

I really hope I get the job.

Speaking and vocabulary

1 **In pairs, discuss the following questions.**

1 What experience do you have of interviews for jobs or college?
2 How do you feel when you have an interview?

2 **a) Look at the *Top Tips for Job Interviews* and complete the sentences using the words in the box.**

experience   long-term goals   promotion prospects
qualifications   references   strengths   weaknesses

b) In pairs, discuss which you think are the three most important tips.

So, how did it go?

Top Tips for Job Interviews

1 Make a list of your _____ – it's important to talk about what you are good at.

2 Make a list of your _____ – interviewers sometimes ask what you are not good at.

3 Prepare to talk about your past _____ – you can talk about things you have done which relate to this job.

4 Make sure you know what relevant _____ you have – certificates, diplomas and degrees are important.

5 Think of two past employers to write you good _____ – the interviewers will need to know about what past employers thought of your work.

6 Show that you are interested in _____ – it's impressive to show interest in getting better jobs in the company in the future.

7 Be clear about your _____ – interviewers sometimes ask what your five-year plan is.

Listening

3 Listen to Madeline telling a friend about her job interview. Answer the questions.

1 How does she think she has done?
2 Was she nervous during the interview?

4 **Listen again and tick (✓) the questions the interviewer asked Madeline.**

1 What experience have you got with this type of work?
2 Why do you want to work here?
3 What are your strengths and weaknesses?
4 What are your long-term goals?
5 Can you work under pressure?
6 What would you do if there was a problem?

Grammar focus

5 Look at the examples of reported questions and complete the rules about word order. Write *main verb* or *subject*.

> A *'What are your strengths?'*
>   **She asked me what** my strengths **were**.
>
> B *'Can you work under pressure?'*
>   **She wanted to know if I could work** under pressure.

1 In Example A (*Wh-* questions):
   She asked me + *question word* + _____ + (modal verb) + _____ .

2 In Example B (*Yes/No* questions):
   She wanted to know + *if* + _____ + (modal verb) + _____ .

6 <u>Underline</u> the correct alternative.

In reported questions, the tense is *the same as/one tense back from* direct questions.

7 Look at the recording script for Exercise 3 on page 123 and find different ways of starting the sentence when reporting questions.

Practice

8 Report these questions. Use different ways of starting the reported questions.

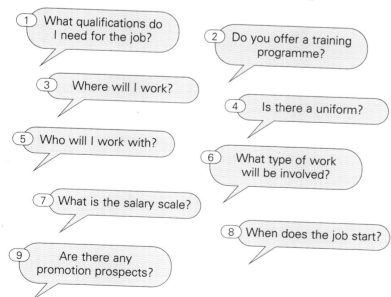

Example:

> What are the responsibilities of the job?

He wanted to know what the responsibilities of the job were.
Or: He asked me what the responsibilities of the job were.

1 What qualifications do I need for the job?

2 Do you offer a training programme?

3 Where will I work?

4 Is there a uniform?

5 Who will I work with?

6 What type of work will be involved?

7 What is the salary scale?

8 When does the job start?

9 Are there any promotion prospects?

> Mum, I got it!

Get talking

9 Report an interview or conversation you have had.

1 Think about a situation when someone asked you questions. It could be about:
   • Jobs – a job interview.
   • Education – a conversation with a teacher or an interview for college / university.
   • Romance – a first date.

2 Report the situation to a partner.
   a) Explain the situation.
   b) How did you feel?
   c) What questions did he / she ask you?

Language to go

A: What did he ask you?
B: He asked me if I wanted the job.

> GRAMMAR REFERENCE PAGE 117
> PRACTICE PAGE 107

Information for pair and group work

Lesson 4, Exercise 8

Name: James Adams
Age: 45
Family: Married, two young children
Job: Marketing manager
Salary: Very high
Qualifications: Company training in sales and marketing

Name: Christine Goldsmith
Age: 48
Family: Single, no children
Job: School head teacher
Salary: High
Qualifications: Degree and post-graduate teaching qualifications

Name: Anna Denton
Age: 38
Family: Single, three children
Job: Secretary with a charity
Salary: Low
Qualifications: None

Lesson 5, Exercise 3 – answers

1 In general, being left-handed means having a dominant right side of the brain. This may mean a preferred hand, foot or eye (for example, with cameras).
2 The ability to use both hands with equal skill and coordination.
3 It depends how you define 'left-handed'. But the percentage in Britain is somewhere between 13% and 30%.
4 Scientists are unsure (though left-handedness appears in some families).

Lesson 15, Exercise 9, Student A

- You can speak English well in class. But when you spend time on the phone, everything goes wrong.
- The office photocopier is a real waste of resources. How can we use less paper?
- Your colleagues always arrive late for meetings. You waste your time waiting for them. Help!

Lesson 6, Exercise 9, Student A

You are the director of Sweets 'R' Us – a big company that makes chocolates. Prepare to have a meeting with a sales representative from a security company. Explain your problems below and see if he / she has any products that can help you. You have a budget of £10,000 to spend.

Lesson 9, Exercise 4, Group B

D _____
If you like outdoor activities, you can canoe up Katherine Gorge or ride camels at Uluru. One of the best ways to see the outback is to walk. If you want to go camping, you'll find that many tour companies offer camping safaris.

E _____
If you prefer some indoor activities, you won't be disappointed either. The Araluen Arts Centre in Alice Springs has a cinema, theatre, opera and galleries. You can also see beautiful examples of ancient aboriginal art.

F _____
Wear boots for walking – Australia has the most dangerous snakes in the world. The sun is very strong for most of the year, so you should use high-factor sun cream and wear a hat. It's also sensible to carry plenty of water with you.

Lesson 14, Exercise 3, Group A

1 What unusual people are at the wedding?
2 What is traditional about the wedding?
3 What is unusual about the bride and groom?

At first sight, it looks like any other wedding. A smart hotel, relatives in hats and new clothes, nervous bridesmaids. But, look again. There are more video cameras and press photographers than usual. There are 25 security guards with hidden microphones and the logo of a radio station on the wall. The radio station has made a great effort to create a genuine traditional wedding with the flowers, guests and beautiful wedding dress. However, it is not a traditional wedding in every sense. The wedding is in three minutes and the bride and groom haven't actually met yet! They have never seen photos of each other and they have only talked on the phone for 40 seconds the day before the wedding.

Sweets 'R' Us

memo

- 30% increase in phone bills – staff making long personal calls?
- Two members of staff were robbed leaving work – no lights in car park.
- 10% of chocolates disappear each week in the packing department – maybe staff are eating them, but no evidence.
- Saw the Sales Manager playing computer games – how many other people do this?

Lesson 18, Exercise 9, Student A

1 You need to borrow money to buy lunch. Ask your friend (Student B).
2 You need to leave work early today. Ask the boss (Student B).
3 You don't want to go into town by bus. Ask a friend (Student B) for a lift in his / her car.
4 You're at the theatre. Someone (Student B) is in your seat. Ask him / her to move.
5 A stranger (Student B) stops you in the street. Listen and reply.
6 Your son / daughter (Student B) has something to ask you. Listen and reply.
7 You are a teacher. One of your students (Student B) has a question for you. Listen and reply.
8 You are at a café. A stranger (Student B) is about to speak to you. Listen and reply.

Lesson 22, Exercise 10, Student A

Look at your information and decide what questions you need to ask Student B in order to complete the information about Venus and Serena Williams. Student B will also ask questions.

1 Venus Williams was born in _____. (When … ?)
2 When the girls were only three years old, they were taught to play tennis by their father, Richard.
3 Their father learned about tennis by _____. (How … ?)
4 They are managed and coached by their father.
5 They have been given the names _____ by the press. (What … ?)
6 Venus is sometimes called 'unfriendly' and 'arrogant' by other competitors.
7 Venus's serve was recorded at _____ – the women's world record. (How fast … ?)
8 Justine Henin was defeated in the women's singles final to make Venus the Wimbledon 2001 champion.

Lesson 24, Exercise 9

SITUATION 1

Student A | Student B

1 You are the receptionist at a bank. Answer the phone.

2 You are a customer. There is a problem with your account. Ask to speak to the manager.

3 Apologise and say he is not in the office.

4 Ask for the manager to contact you later. Give your phone number.

5 Agree to this.

6 Say goodbye.

7 Say goodbye and hang up.

Lesson 28, Exercise 4, Group B

Read the text below. Are the sentences true (T) or false (F)?

1 Winnie Mandela was allowed to be in the same room as her husband during her visits.
2 The prison warders did not lie about the time.
3 They could kiss goodbye.
4 Nelson Mandela remembered the visits in lots of detail.

Visiting Robben Island was not easy. We were allowed to have visits of thirty minutes maximum, and political prisoners were not allowed contact visits, in which the visitor and prisoner were in the same room. The visiting room was small and windowless. One sat in a chair and looked through the thick glass that had a few small holes into it to allow conversation. We had to talk very loudly to be heard.

Suddenly, I heard the warder behind me say, 'Time up! Time up!' I turned and looked at him. It was impossible that half an hour had passed. But, in fact, he was right; visits always seemed to go by in the blink of an eye. For all the years that I was in prison, I never failed to be surprised when the warder called, 'Time up!' My wife, Winnie, and I were both hurried from our chairs and we waved a quick farewell. As I walked back to the cell, I reviewed in my head what we had talked about. Over the next days, weeks, and months, I would return to that one visit again and again. I knew I would not be able to see my wife again for at least six months.

Lesson 30, Exercise 11, Group A

My house plants were dry and needed water this morning. This means bright sunshine and dry weather is coming. And we must always expect good weather when there is no 'r' in the month. This is the middle of July so I confidently expect warm and sunny conditions for next week.

SITUATION 2

Student A | Student B

1 Phone your friend Debbie at her home.

2 You are Debbie's flatmate. Say she is out. Say where.

3 Say you are returning her call.

4 Say when Debbie will be home. Suggest Debbie calls back later. Ask when.

5 Say when you can be contacted. Give your phone number.

6 Say you will ask Debbie to call back then.

7 Say thanks and goodbye.

8 Say goodbye.

Lesson 30, Exercise 11, Group B

> I saw two black cats walking across the road together yesterday. One of them looked straight at me and moved its head slowly up and down. The last time I saw that, there was a heavy thunderstorm within 48 hours. And I've been getting pains in my fingers – that's another sign of wet weather.

Lesson 34, Exercise 9, Student A

PART 1
Prepare what you are going to say to the doctor (Student B) about your symptoms.

Situation 1 Throwing up a lot
Situation 2 High fever for two days
Situation 3 Came out in spots last night
Situation 4 Stomachache

PART 2
You are now the doctor. Listen to Student B's symptoms and offer advice below.

Situation 5 Take some pain killers (e.g. aspirin)
Situation 6 Put hand in cold water to help swelling
Situation 7 Put cream on itchy skin
Situation 8 Have an X-ray

Lesson 15, Exercise 9, Student B

- You have a computer but you're no good at using technology. It feels like you're wasting opportunities!
- You can't remember how to use English modal verbs! You want some good advice.
- Your colleagues spend too long having lunch. You have to waste your time and energy answering the phone.

Lesson 18, Exercise 9, Student B

1 Your friend (Student A) has a request. Listen and reply.
2 Your employee (Student A) has a question for you. Listen and reply.
3 Your friend (Student A) has something to ask you. Listen and reply.
4 You are at the theatre. A stranger (Student A) is about to speak to you. Listen and reply.
5 You don't know where the supermarket is. Ask someone (Student A) in the street.
6 You're going away for the weekend. Ask your Mum / Dad (Student A) to feed your dog.
7 You haven't done your homework. Ask the teacher (Student A) if you can do it tonight.
8 You want to sit down in a café. There's only one free seat. Ask Student A if you can share the table.

Lesson 38, Exercise 11

'Don't worry, be happy' by Bobby McFerrin

Here's a little song I wrote
You might want to sing it note for note
Don't worry, be happy

In every life we have some trouble
But when you worry you make it double
Don't worry, be happy
Don't worry, be happy now

Don't worry, be happy. Don't worry, be happy.
Don't worry, be happy. Don't worry, be happy.

Ain't got no place to lay your head
Somebody came and took your bed
Don't worry, be happy
The landlord say your rent is late
He may have to litigate
Don't worry, be happy
Don't worry, be happy

Don't worry, be happy. Don't worry, be happy.
Don't worry, be happy. Don't worry, be happy.

Lesson 6, Exercise 9, Student B

You are a sales representative from *Safe & sound*, a security company. Your products are listed below. Prepare to have a meeting with the director of a chocolate company. First, find out his / her needs. Then try to sell your products. Remember to explain what they can do / prevent.

SAFE & SOUND Product List

• **'Light up'** – a security light that comes on when it senses movement.	£5,000
• **'Call stopper'** – a device that stops telephone calls to 'unauthorised' numbers.	£3,000
• **'Micro cam'** – a tiny (1cm x 1cm) video camera.	£2,500
• **'Stop IT now!'** – latest technology to prevent computer users from using certain kind of software (e.g. games).	£2,000

Lesson 14, Exercise 3, Group B

1 Why are Carla and Greg getting married?
2 Who is paying for the wedding?
3 How do they feel about the wedding?

Three months ago, Carla (23) and Greg (28) won a competition on a Birmingham radio station. The prize? Each other. And a £50,000 white wedding in a smart hotel, a honeymoon in the Bahamas, an expensive car and a two-bedroom flat for a year. It was called a 'scientific experiment of love'.

Arranged marriages in other cultures can be successful. But it is hard to imagine what kind of person would marry someone that a radio station chooses for them. Carla says, 'I know this is a mad thing to do. But Greg sounds like the kind of man I'd be happy with.' Greg seems genuinely hopeful of finding true love today. He says, 'I've had lots of girlfriends, but it's never worked out. I actually think it's safer to have someone chosen for you than to choose for yourself.'

Lesson 34, Exercise 9, Student B

PART 1
You are a doctor. Listen to Student A's symptoms and offer advice below.

Situation 1 Drink a lot of water
Situation 2 Stay in bed
Situation 3 Don't eat anything
Situation 4 Put cream on the spots

PART 2
You are now the patient – prepare what you are going to say to the doctor (Student A) about your symptoms.

Situation 5 Left hand is aching
Situation 6 Fingers are swollen
Situation 7 Skin is very itchy
Situation 8 Passed out twice with the pain

Lesson 30, Exercise 11, Part 3

The actual weather:

There was a mixture of sun and rain. The result was thick fog which covered the country for 24 hours. Driving conditions were extremely dangerous and people were advised to stay at home. The temperatures were low. But better weather is expected.

Lesson 30, Exercise 11, Group C

The satellite shows a very variable picture. The heavy rain from last week is still with us and many areas can expect winds and light showers. However, there are signs of good weather on the way. Temperatures may rise from tomorrow so there will be a risk of fog – perhaps even thick fog – in some parts.

Lesson 15, Exercise 9, Student C

- You're unfit and need to do more exercise. But running seems a waste of energy. Any ideas?
- You never remember your friends' birthdays. OK, it saves money on cards and presents. But what's the answer?
- You never have enough money at the end of the month. You want to spend less and save more, but how?

Lesson 22, Exercise 10, Student B

Look at your information and decide what questions you need to ask Student A in order to complete the information about Venus and Serena Williams. Student A will also ask questions.

1 Venus Williams was born in June 1980.
2 When the girls were only _____ years old they were taught to play tennis by their father, Richard. (How …?)
3 Their father learned about tennis by watching videos and reading books.
4 They are managed and coached by_____. (Who …?)
5 They have been given the names 'Slice Girls' and 'Sister Act' by the press.
6 Venus is sometimes called _____ and _____ by other competitors. (What … ?)
7 Venus's serve was recorded at 127 mph – the women's world record.
8 _____ was defeated in the women's singles final to make Venus the Wimbledon 2001 champion. (Who …?)

Lesson 38, Exercise 3 – answers

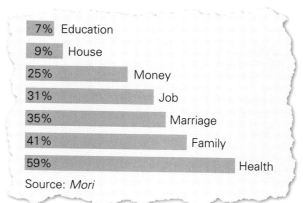

7%	Education
9%	House
25%	Money
31%	Job
35%	Marriage
41%	Family
59%	Health

Source: *Mori*

87

Practice

1 It's absolutely true!

Vocabulary: adjectives and intensifiers

1 Complete the puzzle by following the clues.

1 That film is absolutely *awful* – don't go to see it. (5)
2 I need to go to bed. I'm absolutely _____ ! (9)
3 There were no free seats on the bus. It was very _____ . (7)
4 He's got very _____ feet, hasn't he? (3)
5 I take size 12, not 18. This is absolutely _____ ! (8)
6 65,000 people at the football match – it was absolutely _____ ! (6)
7 After the journey the boys were really _____ . (5)
8 Your party was absolutely _____ . Thank you! (9)

```
      1 | A | W | F | U | L |
  2 |   |   |   |   |   |   |
          3 |   |   |   |   |   |   |
      4 |   |   |   |   |
  5 |   |   |   |   |   |   |
      6 |   |   |   |   |   |
      7 |   |   |   |   |
  8 |   |   |   |   |   |   |   |
```

Grammar: past simple and continuous

2 Underline the correct form of the verbs.

Example: He *took* / *was taking* a shower when I *phoned* / *was phoning* him.

1 We *stopped* / *were stopping* at a café when we *drove* / *were driving* home.
2 I *laughed* / *was laughing* at the photos so much, I *dropped* / *was dropping* my drink.
3 My boyfriend *arrived* / *was arriving* just as I *served* / *was serving* dinner.
4 Someone *took* / *was taking* my wallet while I *got* / *was getting* onto the train.
5 I *danced* / *was dancing* when my shoe *broke* / *was breaking*.

3 Complete the text. Use the correct form of the verbs in brackets.

Sharon likes playing jokes on people. One day, she *went* (go) shopping with her boyfriend Dave. They [1] _____ (walk) around a shop when Sharon [2] _____ (decide) to play a joke on Dave. She [3] _____ (tell) the security guards that Dave [4] _____ (steal) things from the shop. While he [5] _____ (look) at a stereo system, the security guards [6] _____ (arrest) him and [7] _____ (take) him into the manager's office. While they [8] _____ (examine) his pockets, Sharon [9] _____ (laugh).

2 Are you a morning person?

Vocabulary: sleep

1 Correct the mistakes in the following sentences.

Example: Max is a morning ~~man.~~ ✗ *person*

1 Leila wants a lie on.
2 Walter wakes himself up early.
3 Ellie is an early risser.
4 Sam sometimes sleepsover and is late for work.
5 Mandy had an early bed last night.
6 Ronald got out of the bed on the wrong side.
7 Kurt can't keep his eyes awake.
8 Stella likes to stays up late to watch films.

Grammar: subject and object questions

2 Write the words in the correct order to make questions. Add *do* / *does* / *did* if necessary.

Example: in / the / what / Italy? / you / say / morning / in
What do you say in the morning in Italy?

1 Italians / language / speak? / what
_____

2 the / built / Colosseum? / who
_____

3 from? / where / pasta / come
_____

4 Vatican? / lives / the / in / who
_____

5 where / play? / Roma football team
_____

6 Italians / breakfast? / what / drink / for
_____

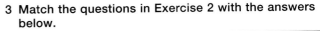

3 Match the questions in Exercise 2 with the answers below.

a) Coffee   b) Buon giorno   c) Italian   d) Italy
e) In Rome   f) The Pope   g) The Romans

Example: *What do you say in the morning in Italy? Buon giorno.*

1 _____   2 _____   3 _____   4 _____   5 _____   6 _____

3 What's in a name?

Vocabulary: associations

1 Complete the sentences with the correct words or phrases in the box.

a) after the American city   b) you   c) chocolate
d) think of chocolate   e) strong image
f) American associations   g) me of New York
h) like American cities

Example: I love your dress – it really suits *you* .

1 The word *Mars* always makes me _____ .
2 I always think 'apple pie' has _____ .
3 Reno and Dallas sound _____ .
4 I drive a big American car because it creates a
 _____ .
5 When people say 'apple', it reminds _____ .
6 Peanuts taste good with _____ .
7 My dog's name is Charlotte – I called her _____ .

Grammar: future with *will* and *going to*

2 Correct the mistakes in the following sentences.

Example: I can't see you tonight because I ~~will~~ go to the cinema. ✗ *'m going to*

1 She booked the flight. She going to go to Spain.
2 I don't think I buy it now, thanks.
3 We've decided. We'll call her Petra.
4 Aren't you going take that new job?
5 Does he will go with us, or not?
6 I not think they're going to go.
7 OK, then. Tell Amy I meet her later.

3 Underline the correct form of the verb.

Example: A: Has Nicky decided on a name for her baby?
 B: Yes. She *will call / 's going to call* him Tom.

1 A: *Will you see / Are you going to see* that band?
 B: Yes, *I will / I am*.
2 A: What *will you give / are you going to give* her for her birthday?
 B: I don't know yet. *I'll think / I'm going to think* about it.
3 A: I've decided – *I'm going to have / I'll have* chicken. And you?
 B: Well … I think *I'm going to have / I'll have* fish.
4 A: It's agreed. *We'll get / We're going to get* married in June.
 B: *Will you have / Are you going to have* a church wedding?
5 A: *I'll go shopping / I'm going to go shopping* with Vera.
 B: Oh, good idea. *I'm going to come / I'll come* too.
6 A: *Are you going to go / Will you go* out tonight?
 B: No, *I won't / I'm not* – I'm too busy.

4 Career paths

Vocabulary: education

1 Put the letters in the correct order, then complete the texts.

a) reysivitun   b) koto   c) deapss   d) teg
e) maxes   f) og   g) gerede   h) tefl   i) draseg

When I was at school, I didn't study and I didn't **get** any qualifications. I [1] _____ school and started working in a boring job with very little money. Five years later, I decided to [2] _____ to college. I [3] _____ all my exams again and this time I [4] _____ them all – I was so pleased.

At school, I always got good [5] _____ , so when I went to [6] _____ , I was very upset when I failed all my [7] _____ in the first year. Now I'm in the second year and I want to study harder. At the end of my three years, I really want to get my [8] _____ .

Grammar: comparatives and superlatives

2 Look at the pictures. Write sentences using the prompts below.

Example: Ben – Anna – good grades:
Ben got better grades than Anna.

| Anna | Ben | Carly |

1 Ben – Anna – successful: _____ .
2 Anna – bad grades: _____ .
3 Carly – Ben – high grades: _____ .
4 Carly – good grades: _____ .
5 Anna – successful: _____ .

3 Correct the mistakes in the following sentences.

Example: I am more interested in biology ~~that~~ in chemistry.
✗ *than*

1 Maria is the most fastest swimmer in the team.
2 Your house is a lot biger than mine.
3 The weather is much badder than it was yesterday.
4 Gina is the successfullest person in our class.
5 She's the most good teacher in the whole school.
6 My brother is tallest person in our family.

5 On the other hand

Vocabulary: levels of difficulty

1 Underline the correct word.

Example: The first time you drive a car it feels very *simple* / *complicated.*

1 I lived in Korea for nineteen years, so learning Korean was *no trouble / hard.*
2 With practice, the Internet really does get more and more *straightforward / impossible.*
3 I tried to catch the ball with my left hand, but as I'm right-handed it was quite *a piece of cake / tough.*
4 I cook a lot, so cooking for eight people was basically *no trouble / complicated.*
5 If you revise often, then remembering the right phrase is usually quite *complicated / simple.*

Grammar: modal verbs for ability

2 Complete the text using the words in the box.

are able to   can do   can't read   can use
can't use   Can you   managed to

Being left-handed means you have a dominant right side of the brain and **can do** most things with your left hand. Many left-handers, however, [1] _____ their right hand for some things. A quick test will show if you are left-handed. [2] _____ fold your hands together? If you have the right thumb on top, you're a 'leftie'. Some people [3] _____ do things with both hands equally well. Being ambidextrous is a big advantage over being a 'leftie'. Lefties [4] _____ scissors properly. Occasionally they [5] _____ or write easily. However, it's not all bad news. Many famous lefties have [6] _____ do great things: Leonardo da Vinci, Marilyn Monroe, Oprah Winfrey and Bill Gates to name but a few!

3 Write the words in the correct order.

Example: both able to hands with She's throw
She's able to throw with both hands.

1 food I spicy eat can't

_____

2 is languages My able speak five to dad

_____

3 the haven't see yet baby managed to We

_____

4 wasn't so forgot photos camera I my able to I take any

_____

5 card was expensive pay able but I It by credit to was

_____

6 I finish difficult but was managed to It it

_____

6 Corporate spying

Vocabulary: crime

1 Find eleven words to do with crime. The first has been done for you.

A	S	E	N	T	E	N	C	E
M	U	V	I	O	P	R	O	V
U	S	I	S	M	R	E	M	I
G	P	A	D	M	I	T	M	D
G	E	L	I	A	S	S	I	E
E	C	H	U	R	O	P	Z	N
R	T	E	D	E	N	Y	O	C
A	C	C	U	S	E	E	C	E
T	H	I	E	V	E	S	H	A

Grammar: adverbs of purpose

2 Combine two sentences to make one sentence. Use the words in brackets.

Example: A cup of coffee is good. It will wake you up. (**for**)
A cup of coffee is good for waking you up.

1 I study hard. I want to learn English fast. (**in order to**)

_____

2 She drives carefully. She doesn't want to have an accident. (**so as not to**)

_____

3 Marco carries a dictionary. He can check vocabulary when he's reading. (**for**)

_____

4 Take an umbrella. It might rain. (**in case**)

_____

5 She always carries her phone. She can call her friends. (**so that**)

_____

6 Write it down. You might forget it. (**in case**)

_____

7 I watch the news in English. I get listening practice. (**to**)

_____

3 Rewrite the sentences so they have the same meaning. Use the words in brackets and make any necessary changes.

Example: In summer, I wear a hat because I want my head to keep cool. (**to**)
In summer, I wear a hat to keep my head cool.

1 In winter, I wear a hat because I don't want to get cold. (**in order to**)
2 He leaves his house at 6.30 because he doesn't want to be late for work. (**so as not to**)
3 Take my phone number because you might want to phone me. (**in case**)
4 She needs a computer because she works at home. (**for**)

7 Teamwork

Vocabulary: work

1 Write the letters in the correct order. Then write the phrases in the correct columns.

lapyp for a job   send an *meila*   *georisan* an event
get a *moontipor*   use a *percumot*   write a *trorpe*
work in a *emat*   go for an *tewirevin*   *ecrevei* a fax

getting a different job	using an office machine	other work activities
apply for a job		

Grammar: present perfect simple

2 Underline the correct form of the verbs.

Greg: Hello, my name's Greg Jones. I'd like to apply for the manager's job.
Len: Well, I hope *you had / you've had* the right experience. [1] *Did you do / Have you done* this kind of job before?
Greg: Yes, [2] *I did / I have.*
Len: Where?
Greg: Well [3] *I worked / I've worked* at United Football Club.
Len: Great! Tell me more.
Greg: [4] *I was / I've been* there last year.
Len: OK. But [5] *were you / have you been* the manager last year?
Greg: Well … er … no, [6] *I wasn't / I haven't.*
Len: But we need someone who [7] *had / has had* management experience. And [8] *you didn't / you haven't.*
Greg: No, that's right, [9] *I didn't / I haven't.*
Len: Look, I'm sorry. Try again when [10] *you had / you've had* more experience. Thanks for calling. Goodbye.
Greg: Bye.

3 Correct the mistakes in the sentences. Be careful – not all the sentences are wrong!

Example: Have you ~~gone~~ to China? ✗ *been*

1 Have you ever ated Indian food?
2 He's never worked in an office, did he?
3 I've never been here before.
4 Have you ever lyed to your boss?
5 We've bought a new computer yesterday.
6 Sarah's seen the new team leader. He's gorgeous!
7 They've flown on Concorde in 1999.
8 They ran the London marathon last year.

8 Nice to meet you

Vocabulary: topics of conversation

1 Complete the crossword.

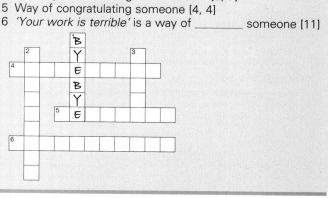

1 Informal way to close a conversation [3-3]
2 Way of introducing Ron to someone else [4, 2, 3]
3 Friendly way to start a conversation [5]
4 Safe topic for 'making conversation' [3, 7]
5 Way of congratulating someone [4, 4]
6 'Your work is terrible' is a way of _____ someone [11]

Function: managing a conversation

2 Write the words in the correct order.

a) is Charlie Frances, this
Frances, this is Charlie .

b) me you everyone introduce let to
_____ .

c) you 1.30 see then at
_____ .

d) and family are your you how
_____ ?

e) again see to good you here
_____ .

f) was journey how the
_____ ?

g) dress I your love
_____ !

h) food but terrible the was
_____ .

3 Write the phrases from Exercise 2 in the correct part of the dialogue.

Jerry: Hello. [1] _____ .
Frances: It's very nice to be here. [2] _____?
Jerry: Very well, thanks. [3] _____? Good flight?
Frances: Not bad. [4] _____.
Jerry: Oh, poor you! Ah … Here are the others.
[5] _____. [6] *Frances, this is Charlie (a)* … and I think you already know Benita, don't you?
Frances: Yes, we met last year.
Benita: I must say [7] _____, Frances.
Frances: Thank you.
Charlie: Anyway, the meeting starts at 2.00. Let's meet again at 1.30 shall we?
Frances: Right. [8] _____.
Jerry: See you later.

> For more exercises, go to www.language-to-go.com **91**

9 Australia

Vocabulary: travel items

1 Reorder the letters to make compound nouns.

a) nair tochels   b) lepsinge gab   c) uns mecra
d) yemno tebl   e) toomsuiq pelelentr   f) tirfs-ida tik
g) gikawln sotbo   h) trawe lobtet   i) ugied kobo

Example: a) *rain clothes*

Grammar: first conditional

2 Choose the correct endings (a–h) for the sentences (1–8).

1 I'll drive this morning.   f
2 We can sit under a tree   —
3 I'll buy some sun cream   —
4 If we go for a walk,   —
5 Put on some mosquito repellent   —
6 If you make a fire,   —
7 Please be careful of snakes   —
8 If you stop here for a minute,   —

a) if we see a shop.
b) if you walk around in the grass.
c) I can take a photograph.
d) unless you want to get bitten.
e) I'll cook dinner.
f) if you drive this afternoon.
g) we'll take some water with us.
h) if it gets too hot.

3 Complete the sentences with the correct form of the verbs in brackets.

Example: If I ___remember___ (remember), ___I'll buy___ (buy) a newspaper.

1 John _____ (be) glad if you _____ (come) to the party.
2 If you _____ (go) in March, the weather _____ (be) perfect.
3 If you _____ (phone) me tonight, I _____ (tell) you the news.
4 What _____ (you / do) if she _____ (not come) to the meeting?
5 Unless you _____ (help) me, I _____ (not finish) it.
6 If the waiter _____ (do) that again, I _____ (ask) to speak to the manager.

10 Take it easy

Vocabulary: expressions with *take*

1 Underline the correct word.

Example: I like doing sports with other people and taking *easy* / *part* / *break* in team games.

1 Everyone can take a *easy* / *part* / *break* for five minutes and have a cup of coffee.
2 Don't take *in* / *off* / *on* any more work – you haven't got time.
3 I've got a hospital appointment on Friday. Can I take the day *on* / *up* / *off* ?
4 You're very tired. Sit down and take it *off* / *easy* / *break*.
5 I need to do more exercise. I think I'll take *on* / *in* / *up* playing tennis.

2 Rewrite the sentences using expressions with *take* to replace the underlined words.

Example: Come on! Relax! Just enjoy yourself!
Come on! Take it easy! Just enjoy yourself!

1 You look ill. Why don't you have a holiday today?
_____ .

2 The exam finishes at 2.30, then you can have some free time for an hour.
_____ .

3 You can do many outdoor activities on this holiday.
_____ .

4 Last year, I tried to do more than was possible and I got very tired.
_____ .

5 I've got more time now, so I'm going to begin a new hobby.
_____ .

Grammar: verb constructions for likes and dislikes

3 Correct the mistakes in the following sentences.

Example: I can't stand ~~to play~~ computer games.
✗ *playing*

1 My brother's really to rollerskating.
2 Are you keen of going to the cinema?
3 I don't mind to do my homework.
4 He feels sick of doing the dishes.
5 Mandy doesn't stand playing the violin.
6 I don't want go to work today.
7 She don't mind walking to wor[k]
8 He isn't keen on watch football.
9 She enjoys to play tennis

11 Determination

Vocabulary: determination

1 Complete the sentences using the correct form of the words in brackets.

Example: Smoking is horrible – I really feel like _giving up_. (give up)

1 I drink coffee every day and it's probably very
_____ ! (addict)
2 You need a lot of _____ to break a habit of a lifetime. (determine)
3 Have you thought about _____ on red meat? (cut down)
4 You need lots of willpower _____ chocolate. (give up)
5 My sister cut down on _____ because she was spending too much. (shop)
6 She's _____ on her mobile phone; she takes it everywhere. (depend)

Grammar: *used to*

2 Complete the sentences using the correct form of *used to*.

Example: I _used to_ live in Spain when I was a child.

1 What time _____ (you) go to bed when you were five?
2 I _____ hate olives, but now I quite like them.
3 What _____ (you) like doing when you were a teenager?
4 He _____ (not) go out much, but now he's never at home!
5 _____ (you) have short hair?
6 We _____ have a piano, but we sold it.

3 Write sentences about Gordon using *used to*.

| 1980 | Today |

Example: student / job _Gordon used to be a student but now he's got a job._

1 live with parents / married
_____.

2 no children / a daughter
_____.

3 have skateboard / a car
_____.

4 play the guitar / play golf
_____.

5 not wear glasses / wear glasses
_____.

12 Money matters

Vocabulary: money and banks

1 Complete the dialogues using the words in the box.

a) deposit b) in the black c) saving d) statement
e) savings f) lend g) borrowed h) interest i) in the red
j) withdrawing k) current

I'm **saving** all my money for my retirement. I've never ¹ _____ any money from my friends or my bank. I think if you can't pay for something you shouldn't buy it. My bank account is never ² _____ . I ³ _____ money into my ⁴ _____ account every month because you know it's safe there and the bank pays me ⁵ _____ , about 6% a year. It all adds up over time you know.

I think you should enjoy life and spend your money while you can. I'm always ⁶ _____ money from my ⁷ _____ account – I never know how much money I've got until the bank sends me a ⁸ _____ . I'm always asking people to ⁹ _____ me money to get back ¹⁰ _____ . It doesn't worry me though – it's only money.

Grammar: verbs with two objects

2 Put the words in the correct order and add any necessary punctuation.

Example: lent bank the me money the
The bank lent me the money.

1 the us they news told
2 Indonesia me present brought a from he
3 you to please show me could it
4 vocabulary taught teacher some my us
5 ask can help for you me always
6 curry order a please me chicken
7 lost she I was so a map me drew
8 me send a to don't postcard forget

13 The river

Vocabulary: phrasal verbs about tourism

1 Rewrite the sentences so they have the same meaning. Use the words in brackets and make any necessary changes.

Example: We left the train at Paddington Station. (get)
We got off the train at Paddington Station.

1 The show was very long – it lasted four hours. (go)

_____ .

2 My car stopped working twice last week. (break)

_____ .

3 Could you give me temporary accommodation tonight? (put)

_____ .

4 We began our journey early so the traffic wasn't very busy. (set)

_____ .

5 There were no more trains that night so I continued by bus. (carry)

_____ .

2 Put the parts of the story in the correct order.

Order: 1 f   2 __   3 __   4 __   5 __   6 __   7 __   8 __

a) down. We waited while the driver tried to fix it. This went

b) us up for the night and we went home the next day.

c) on driving for about three hours. We were hungry by then so we got

d) on for about six hours. He couldn't do it but luckily, a local farmer put

e) off the bus and had a picnic by the road. After lunch, we set

f) It was a long journey so we started

g) off again at about 2.00 p.m. Suddenly, the bus broke

h) off early from our hotel. At 10.00 a.m., we stopped for a drink and then we carried

Grammar: present simple and continuous for future

3 Complete the dialogue using the present simple or present continuous.

Martina: My exams *finish* (finish) at 4.00 on Friday!
Sophia: [1] _____ (you / do) anything nice this weekend?
Martina: Yes, I [2] _____ (meet) some friends on Friday evening. Do you want to come?
Sophia: Oh, no thanks – I [3] _____ (stay) in.
Martina: Are you sure?
Sophia: Yes. I [4] _____ (finish) work at 5.30 and I [5] _____ (go) straight home.
Martina: [6] _____ (you / do) anything on Saturday?
Sophia: Yes – I [7] _____ (go) on a trip to Oxford. The coach [8] _____ (leave) at 8.00.
Martina: That's early.
Sophia: Yes, that's why I [9] _____ (go) to bed early on Friday, because I [10] _____ (get up) at 6.30 on Saturday morning!

14 Radio wedding

Vocabulary 1: weddings

1 Complete the crossword.

1 Man who is getting married. (5)
2 Formal party after a wedding. (9)
3 Man who promises to get married. (6)
4 Wedding that is not in a church. (5)
5 Woman who promises to get married. (7)
6 Man who helps the man who is getting married. (4, 3)
7 Church wedding. (9)
8 Special, formal actions at a wedding. (8)
9 Holiday taken after a wedding. (9)

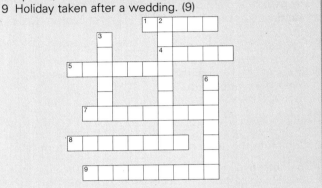

Vocabulary 2: uses of *get*

2 Complete the sentences using the words in the box.

back	know	married	over	with

Example: When my sister got *married*, she wore white.

1 My dog died last year and I still feel sad. I haven't got _____ it yet.
2 My boyfriend and I have separated, but I still love him and want to get _____ together.
3 Choi is my best friend. We get on really well _____ each other.
4 At first he seems unfriendly, but he's really nice when you get to _____ him.

3 Rewrite the sentences using expressions with *get* to replace the underlined words.

Example: My parents <u>became husband and wife</u> 30 years ago.
My parents got married 30 years ago.

1 They had a big party when they <u>agreed to get married</u>.

_____ .

2 I <u>have a friendly relationship with</u> both my sisters.

_____ .

3 She <u>became sad and angry</u> when she failed her exam.

_____ .

4 We lived separately for two months but now we've <u>become partners again</u>.

_____ .

5 We went on holiday and had an opportunity to <u>find out about</u> each other.

_____ .

15 Less is more

Vocabulary: *waste, use, spend, save* + noun

1 Complete the text using the words in the box.

> a) save your energy   b) using your time
> c) use the opportunities   d) wasting time
> e) waste of energy   f) spend some time
> g) save you time

HURRY SICKNESS

Many people are suffering from the 21st century epidemic – *Hurry sickness*.

Sufferers try to fit *everything* into *every* day. They never seem to stop panicking. So remember:

- It's important that you **spend some time** planning your day.
- Try to understand that taking breaks is [1] _____ well.
- Taking the stairs instead of the lift is not [2] _____ .
- Getting angry in a traffic jam is a [3] _____ . It doesn't [4] _____ or get you there faster.
- Don't get impatient waiting for e-mails to download. [5] _____ to worry about the more important things in life.

Dr Jacqueline Atkinson, a psychologist specialising in time management at the University of Glasgow, says that new technology makes it harder for people to control their lives and still have a good quality of life. You should [6] _____ that technology provides, but don't think that it will solve all your problems.

Grammar: modal verbs for giving advice

2 Correct the mistakes in the following sentences.

Example: You should ~~to~~ go away for the weekend sometimes. ✗

1 You no should worry about being late all the time.
2 Perhaps you could trying walking to work.
3 I think you ought to taking more breaks.
4 Perhaps you don't ought to use the car so much.
5 Perhaps could you plan your day better.
6 You should to not eat your lunch at your desk.

3 Give advice for someone who's feeling ill using the words in brackets.

Example: Take an aspirin. (could)
Perhaps you could take an aspirin.

1 Go to the doctor. (should)
_____

2 Don't go to work. (ought to)
_____

3 Stay in bed. (could)
_____

4 Don't get cold. (should)
_____

16 Looks good!

Vocabulary: the five senses

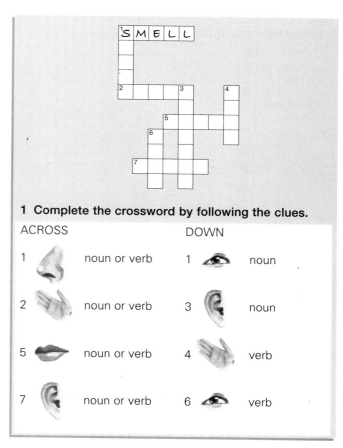

1 Complete the crossword by following the clues.

ACROSS

1 noun or verb
2 noun or verb
5 noun or verb
7 noun or verb

DOWN

1 noun
3 noun
4 verb
6 verb

Grammar: defining relative clauses

2 Complete the sentences using a relative pronoun (if necessary) from the box.

> when   where   which   who   whose   that

Example: It's the restaurant **where** we first kissed.

1 She's someone _____ I met at a party.
2 I remember the time _____ you asked me to dance.
3 I'm the one _____ will make you happy.
4 He's someone _____ heart is very open.
5 You're the one _____ I want.
6 It's our love _____ keeps us together.

3 Combine two sentences to make one. Add a relative pronoun (if necessary) and make any other changes.

Example: She's got a car. It goes at more than 220 km an hour.
She's got a car that goes at more than 220 km an hour.

1 What's the name of that couple? They have six children.
2 Put it in the office. Robert works there.
3 Where's that parcel? It was delivered this morning.
4 There's a film on tonight. You might like it.
5 This is the plane. It carries over 450 people.

17 Changes

Vocabulary: lifestyle: word building

1a) Put the letters in the correct order then match each noun with the correct picture.

| a) sssert   b) dogo thelah   c) ccsssue |
| d) papinsshe   e) einso   f) thwale |

Example: _happiness (d)_   1 _____

2 _____   3 _____

4 _____   5 _____

b) Write the adjective which goes with each noun.

Example: _happiness – happy_

Grammar: present perfect simple with _yet, already, just_

2 Use the prompts to write complete sentences.

a) I / just /do / it _I've just done it_.
b) No / she / move / yet _____ .
c) No thanks. I / already / eat _____ .
d) I / not / know. I / not / read / it / yet _____ .
e) No / I / see / it / recently _____ .
f) Yes / they / decide / make / the changes _____ .

3 Match the answers in Exercise 2 with the questions below.

Example: _1 a_

1 Can you do the ironing for me? _a_
2 Is that a good book? ____
3 Would you like to stay for dinner? ____
4 Have they reached a decision yet? ____
5 Have you seen the cat around here anywhere? ____
6 Has Julia moved house? ____

18 How polite are you?

Vocabulary: phrasal verbs: _turn, switch, go._

1 Correct the mistakes in the sentences. Be careful – not all the sentences are wrong!

Example: When the food's done, turn the cooker ~~on.~~ ✗ _off_

1 I can't hear the TV. Could you turn up it?
2 Mobile phones should not be switched on on aircraft.
3 If you turn off the radio, I can listen to the news.
4 Computers only work if you switch them up.
5 Turn it up! This is the best song on the album.
6 When you go to bed, be sure to turn all the lights on.
7 We switch the heating off at the start of winter.
8 If the air conditioning is too cold, then turn off it.

Function: informal and polite requests

2 Write the words in the correct order.

Example: you bit the window close could a
Could you close the window a bit?

1 mind tomorrow early you coming would ?
_____ .

2 up you a speak can bit ?
_____ .

3 again say could that you ?
_____ .

4 I mind if you now go do ?
_____ .

5 time me could tell the you ?
_____ .

6 me you can the results phone with please ?
_____ .

7 mind you helping homework would with me my ?
_____ .

3 Rewrite the requests to make them more polite.

Example: Open the door!
Would you mind opening the door?

1 Move your car!
Could _____

2 Don't interrupt me again!
Do you mind _____

3 I need to go into town. So give me a lift!
Can _____

4 Don't smoke in here!
Do you mind _____

5 You're making too much noise!
Please could _____

6 Wait for me!
Would you mind _____

19 Going alone

Vocabulary: adjectives describing loneliness and fear

1a) Find five adjectives in the wordsquare. The first has been done for you.

A	L	L	O	N	Y	L
W	O	R	R	I	E	D
I	L	S	E	R	V	A
L	O	C	H	A	S	E
O	N	A	I	L	P	T
N	E	R	V	O	U	S
R	L	E	W	N	I	E
L	Y	D	O	E	R	R

b) Match the words with the definitions below.

Example: Full of fear, very frightened. = *scared*

1 Unhappy because of being alone or without friends.
2 Separated from others.
3 An uncomfortable feeling about a specific experience (e.g. an exam).
4 An uncomfortable feeling about a general idea (e.g. flying).

Grammar: second conditional

2 Complete the dialogue with the correct form of the verbs.

Arek: How <u>would you feel</u> (you / feel) if you
1 _____ (get) stuck in a lift?
Dave: If the doors ² _____ (not open), I ³ _____ (not panic). I ⁴ _____ (try) and stay calm. If I ⁵ _____ (have) a phone with me, I ⁶ _____ (phone) for help. What ⁷ _____ (you / do)?
Arek: Oh, I really hate small spaces. I ⁸ _____ (not be) calm at all. If I really ⁹ _____ (be) stuck, I think I ¹⁰ _____ (scream).

3 Write sentences using the second conditional. Begin with the words in the brackets.

Example: I haven't got his address. I want to send him an e-mail. (If …)
If I had his address, I'd send him an e-mail.

1 He hasn't got time. He wants to finish the report today. (If …)
2 I want to buy a horse. I live in a city. (I …)
3 I don't study very hard. I always fail my exams. (If …)
4 I'm not very rich. I don't know the winning lottery numbers. (I …)
5 I don't have a yacht. I can't go sailing at weekends. (If …)
6 I want to do things differently. I can't live my life over again. (I …)

20 In the fridge

Vocabulary: food and cooking

1 Correct the mistakes in the following sentences.

Example: I can't eat this soup – my ~~fork~~ is dirty. ✗ *spoon*

1 My father is a cooker in a restaurant.
2 It will be a three-plate dinner: soup, meat and dessert.
3 What time do you have your biggest menu of the day?
4 My sister is a vegan, so she eats a lot of eggs.
5 You should always keep ice cream in the frozen.
6 I used to be a vegetable, but now I eat meat and fish.
7 Put the carrots in water and fry them for ten minutes.

Grammar: verb constructions with *-ing* / infinitives

2 Underline the correct form of the verbs.

Example: I've decided <u>*to do*</u> / *doing* a computer course.

1 He usually avoids **to eat** / **eating** any meat products.
2 I can't afford **to buy** / **buying** new clothes every month.
3 Tom is going to give up **smoking** / **to smoke**.
4 She managed **to pass** / **passing** all her exams.
5 You waste so much time **to play** / **playing** computer games.
6 They're planning **to have** / **having** a surprise party for Megan.
7 I offered **to clear up** / **clearing up** after dinner.
8 He keeps on **to interrupt** / **interrupting** me.

3 Complete the text with the correct form of the verb in brackets.

Simple solutions
FOR A NEW YOU

Try these three fabulous ideas from our new beauty editor, Sarah Foster.

FITTER

• You'll look good if you decide <u>*to do*</u> (do) more exercise. Don't spend time ¹ _____ (talk) about it. Join a gym and make sure you manage ² _____ (go) there regularly.

FRESHER

• Think of the money you'll save if you give up ³ _____ (smoke). Don't just keep on ⁴ _____ (say) you're going to give up, but really do it. It's easier if you avoid ⁵ _____ (go) to places where other people smoke.

FRIENDLIER

• Go out more. You probably waste a lot of time ⁶ _____ (watch) TV. Plan ⁷ _____ (meet) friends after work. Go somewhere you enjoy. You can afford ⁸ _____ (be) nice to yourself.

We can't promise miracles but we offer ⁹ _____ (make) your life more fun!

21 Airport

Vocabulary: travel and airports

1 Put the letters in the correct order. Then match the words to the correct definition.

> a) driangbo drac   b) opsspart troconl
> c) yutd erfe poshs   d) kechc-ni kesd   e) nicab wrec
> f) nhad ggalueg   g) petdeaurr goulen
> h) htiflg mofinratnoi necress

Example: *1 e – cabin crew*

1 The people who look after you on an airplane.
2 Where you wait to get on the plane.
3 Where you go to say you've arrived.
4 You can't get on the plane without one.
5 Where you buy cheaper alcohol and cigarettes.
6 Where you see what time your plane goes.
7 Where they check your passport.
8 The bags you carry onto the plane.

Grammar: past perfect simple

2 Underline the correct form of the verbs.

Example: When she *finished* / *had finished* three sandwiches, she *felt* / *had felt* better.

1 When I *arrived* / *'d arrived*, the concert *already started* / *had already started*.
2 We *wanted* / *had wanted* some lunch, but the restaurant *didn't open* / *hadn't opened*.
3 I realised that I *forgot* / *'d forgotten* my keys, when I *pushed* / *'d pushed* the door.
4 I *wanted* / *'d wanted* to buy the jeans that I *saw* / *'d seen* the day before.
5 When Peter came in, he *realised* / *'d realised* that we *organised* / *'d organised* a surprise party.

3 Put these events in the correct order.

a) I was late for the meeting   __
b) I realised that I had missed a bus   __
c) after I had waited forty minutes for the next one __
d) when I arrived at the bus stop   *1*

a) the train wasn't there   __
b) when I looked at my ticket   __
c) I saw that the train had left at 8.45   __
d) when I arrived at the station at 9.45   __

22 A star is born … or made?

Vocabulary: adjectives and nouns to describe fame and success

1 Form the correct adjective from the noun in brackets.

Example: A *famous* film star moved into my village. FAME

1 She is really _____ – all the critics agree on that. SKILL
2 I think she is _____ in her roles. BRILLIANCE
3 That group is really _____ at the moment. FASHION
4 The _____ idea came from her father. ORIGIN
5 Hundreds came and it was very _____. SUCCESS
6 Robert de Niro's a really _____ actor. TALENT

Grammar: passive constructions

2 Complete the texts with the correct form of the verb in brackets. Be careful – not all the verbs are in the passive.

Great Inventions

The ice lolly *was created* (create) by an American called Frank Epperson. He was a lemonade salesman and he discovered ice lollies by accident! He [1] _____ (leave) a glass of lemonade with a spoon in it outside his house on a freezing cold night. When Epperson [2] _____ (find) the glass in the morning, he tried to take the spoon out. But the lemonade [3] _____ (freeze) during the night and it came out of the glass on the spoon. So the first ice lolly [4] _____ (invent). The idea [5] _____ (sell) to a food processing company. Ice lollies [6] _____ (know) as 'popsicles' in the USA.

Vespas The first commercially successful scooter, the Vespa, [7] _____ (made) in 1946 by the Italian company Piaggio. It was a new kind of vehicle: a two-wheeled personal transport. The frame was open, the two small wheels could easily [8] _____ (remove) and a passenger could [9] _____ (carry) on the back. The Vespa was practical and economical and millions of people [10] _____ (buy) them. Today it [11] _____ (see) as the best of city fashion.

23 The future of toys

Vocabulary: toys and games

1 Write the letters in the correct order and match them with the pictures.

a) besatodark   b) gajwis zuzepl   c) droba mega
d) radsc   e) losdl   f) petcromu mage

1	2
3	4
5	6

Grammar: modal verbs to talk about future probability

2 Correct the mistakes in the following sentences.

Example: He may not ~~to go~~ to the party on Saturday. ✗ *go*

1 I don't might take the exam this year.
2 I'm sure you might like the new job.
3 I doubt if he arrives late.
4 He don't think it'll rain tomorrow.
5 We won't to go without you.
6 I'll expect I'll go by train.

3 Rewrite the sentences so they have the same meanings. Use the modal verb in brackets and make any necessary changes.

Example: It's possible that people will use phones less and e-mail more. **(might)**
People might use phones less and e-mail more.

1 I don't know if John will be late today. **(might)**
2 I'm sure I want to be a scientist or a doctor. **(will)**
3 He hasn't decided if he's going skiing this year. **(might)**
4 It's impossible that my boss will cancel the meeting. **(will)**
5 It's possible that Anne will be able to help you. **(may)**
6 I haven't decided if I'll go on studying English. **(might)**
7 He's not sure whether to phone the doctor today. **(may)**
8 There's a possibility that the job starts on Monday. **(could)**

24 I'll call you

Vocabulary: telephoning expressions

1 Complete the puzzle and find the mystery word.

1 If someone isn't there when I phone, I always leave a **message**. (7)
2 Please don't _____ up – I just want to ask you a question. (4)
3 Hi, _____ is Julia Williams speaking. (4)
4 Oh, could you _____ the phone for me? (6)
5 _____ people on your mobile is really good fun. (7)
6 Can you ask John to _____ my call, please. (6)
7 For details of future events, please _____ two. (5)
8 I want to use the _____ but it's broken. Have you got a mobile? (3, 5)
9 I always carry my _____ with me, so people can contact me. (6)
10 She spends so much time talking _____ the phone. (2)
11 I've got three phone calls to _____ this afternoon. (4)

```
¹M E S S A G E
  ²
 ³
 ⁴
    ⁵
     ⁶
     ⁷
⁸
    ⁹
    ¹⁰
 ¹¹
```

Grammar: phrasal verbs about telephoning.

2 Write the words in the correct order.

Example: speaking hello Julio it's
Hello, it's Julio speaking

1 A: it's can speak Ana hi to I Rita
  B: not moment at she's I'm here afraid the

2 A: message a leave please can I
  B: course of Yes

3 A: manager speak I'd to to the hello please like
  B: here speaking if hold see I'll he's who's on

4 A: Jun Fuji his returning it's I'm call
  B: through and now put I'll you try

5 A: the the busy moment at line's I'm afraid
  B: call in later that I'll back him case

> For more exercises, go to www.language-to-go.com **99**

Practice

25 Do the right thing

Vocabulary: *make* and *do*

1 Complete the text using *make* or *do*.

First Impressions Count

You meet someone for the first time. You want to <u>make</u> a good impression but you are not exactly sure what to ¹ _____ .

First, ² _____ sure that the other person feels relaxed. It's good not to look too serious, so remember to smile.

³ _____ your best to listen carefully to what he or she is saying. Everyone likes a good listener.

Another thing is to ⁴ _____ a point of learning his or her name. Once remembered, don't forget to use it!

You can't always ⁵ _____ the right thing, but you can easily ⁶ _____ those first impressions more positive.

Grammar: modal verbs for necessity and obligation

2 Match the situations with the correct sentence.

1 Driving a car   f
2 You've been arrested   __
3 In an exam   __
4 In a job interview   __
5 A friend tells you a secret   __
6 In a library   __

a) You must remember to ask some questions.
b) You have to speak quietly.
c) You mustn't tell anyone.
d) You don't have to say anything.
e) You should read the questions carefully.
f) You must wear a seat belt.

3 Rewrite the sentences so they have the same meanings. Start with the word(s) given.

Example: It's New Year and I feel it's necessary for me to make some changes.
It's New Year and I *must make some changes.*

1 It's not necessary for me to get up early on Saturday.
I _____ .

2 It's a good idea to try to remember friends' birthdays.
You _____ .

3 It's prohibited to copy other students' answers in exams.
We _____ .

4 It's not necessary to pay for library books – they're free.
You _____ .

5 My teacher says that it's necessary for me to do more homework.
My teacher says that I _____ .

6 It's forbidden to drink and drive.
You _____ .

26 Six and a half hours

Vocabulary: expressions with *time*

1 Correct the mistakes in the following sentences.

Example: Sorry I'm late – the journey took a long ~~of~~ time today. ✗

1 I hate being late, so I make sure that my journeys are carefully timing.
2 I had really good time at the office party.
3 I think that sitting in a traffic jam is a waste off time.
4 I love having time out, when I don't have to go to work.
5 By time I get home from work, I'm exhausted.
6 I always arrive for work on the time.

Grammar: ways to express contrasting ideas

2 Complete the sentences using *although*, *however*, *in spite of*, *despite* or *despite not*.

Example: He felt ill. <u>However</u> , he went to work.

1 He went to work, _____ feeling ill.
2 _____ it rained every day, we enjoyed our holiday.
3 _____ feeling hungry, she ate an enormous meal.
4 _____ the coat was expensive, it was worth it.
5 The film was a critical success. _____, it didn't make any money.
6 _____ being lonely, she never felt sad.
7 He failed the exam, _____ all the studying he did.

3 You have some problems with one of your employees. Write sentences telling him / her about the problems. Use the words in brackets.

Example: Work starts at 8.00. You are often late. (although)
Although work starts at 8.00, you are often late.

1 The morning break is fifteen minutes. You take twenty. (however)
_____

2 Lunch finishes at 12.30. You never come back on time. (although)
_____

3 This is a non-smoking office. You smoke all the time. (in spite of)
_____

4 There are three weeks paid holiday. You take extra time off. (however)
_____

5 Employees cannot make personal phone calls. You make a lot. (although)
_____

6 Work doesn't finish until 5.30. You always leave early. (despite not)
_____

27 Achievement

Vocabulary: achievements and projects

1 Complete the crossword. All the answers are nouns.

Across
1 difficulty that needs attention (7)
6 document, made by an official person, which says that the facts are true (11)
7 something given for success in a competition or race (5)
8 spoken or written test of knowledge (11)

Down
1 piece of work that needs careful planning over a period of time (7)
2 strong desire for success (8)
3 special ability to do something well (5)
4 important job in a hospital (6)
5 piece of equipment for a particular purpose (6)

¹P	R	O	B	L	E	M

2 Write the letters of the verbs in the correct order. Then match them with the nouns from Exercise 1.

Example: to (kowr) <u>work</u> on <u>a project</u>

1 to (heaviec) _____
2 to (crievee) _____
3 to (nwi) _____
4 to (vesrie) _____ for _____
5 to (narit) _____ to be _____
6 to (pedlove) _____
7 to (vennit) _____
8 to (lesov) _____

Grammar: present perfect simple and continuous

3 Complete the sentences using the correct form of the present perfect.

Example: I <u>'ve planted</u> (plant) two new trees in my garden.

1 They _____ (play) tennis all afternoon.
2 _____ (you reach) level three on that new computer game?
3 My mother _____ (cook) all morning.
4 Look, she _____ (make) all these cakes.
5 I _____ (try) to fix my car but it still doesn't work.
6 I feel really fit because I _____ (go) to the gym three times a week.
7 You look exhausted! _____ (you run)?

28 Long walk to freedom

Function: prohibition, obligation and permission in the past

1 Put the words in the right order, then match the sentences with the signs.

Example: by everyone They leave midnight made
<u>They made everyone leave by midnight. – Sign A</u>

1 anybody They bar let gamble in didn't the
2 had People to off dirty their boots take
3 made outside guns leave their They men
4 let children place didn't They any the in
5 to kept had Horses outside be

2 Complete the dialogue between Joana and Suzie using the prompts.

J: What a nightmare flight!
S: Why? What happened?
J: Well, first they said I had too much luggage. They <u>didn't let me take</u> (let / take) my three suitcases on to the plane without paying.
S: How much ¹ _____ (have / pay)?
J: Actually, the man was quite kind. He ² _____ (make / pay) for all of it. In the end, I only ³ _____ (have / pay) for one extra suitcase.
S: Oh, well. That's not so bad.
J: No, but I wanted to bring my dog. But I ⁴ _____ (allow / bring) him because he didn't have a passport.
S: A passport? For your dog?
J: Yes, they ⁵ _____ (make / leave) him at the airport.
S: You didn't leave him there, did you?
J: No, they ⁶ _____ (let / phone) my friend and she came and took him home.
S: Oh, that's good. So, everything was OK in the end.
J: Well, yes. Except the plane was three hours late!
S: Oh, poor you! What an awful trip!

29 Shaking hands

Vocabulary: doing business

1 Tick (✓) the *two* correct endings for each verb.

Example: I made …   a) contact. ✔
                   b) a lot of money. ✔
                   c) business. ✘

1 He offered me …   a) to go to dinner. ☐
                   b) a bribe. ☐
                   c) a cup of coffee. ☐

2 We exchanged …   a) telephone numbers. ☐
                  b) my e-mail address. ☐
                  c) business cards. ☐

3 He arranged …   a) the suitcase. ☐
                b) the wedding. ☐
                c) a meeting. ☐

4 They negotiated …   a) a good deal. ☐
                  b) a cheap price. ☐
                  c) an appointment. ☐

5 I did …   a) a good impression. ☐
              b) business with him. ☐
              c) my best. ☐

6 She went on …   a) a business trip. ☐
                b) a meeting. ☐
              c) for an hour. ☐

Grammar: First and second conditionals

2 Match the first and second parts of the sentences.

1 If the company went on-line,   *d*
2 If I win the race,   ___
3 If I was the new boss,   ___
4 You won't be late   ___
5 He'll be sick   ___
6 If you vote for me,   ___
7 He'd be sick   ___

a) if you get up early.
b) if he knew we were in Hawaii.
c) if you give him another chocolate.
d) it'd help sales.
e) I'd increase all our salaries.
f) I'll promise to help the poor.
g) I'll be the school champion.

3 Write first or second conditional sentences about the situations.

Example: It's likely that the meeting will finish late.
I want to get a taxi. (If …)
If the meeting finishes late, I'll get a taxi.

1 I'll probably get a pay rise next week. I want to buy a new TV. (If …)
2 It's very unlikely that he'll fail his exam. He wants to take it again. (If …)
3 I want to go to the party but I feel really sick. (I …)
4 I'm sure that it'll rain tomorrow. I don't want to walk to work in the rain. (If …)
5 He wants to send her an e-mail but he doesn't know her e-mail address. (He…)

30 Sunshine and showers

Vocabulary: the weather

1 Complete the sentences with words from the two boxes.

Adjectives		Nouns	
bright	heavy	cloud	snow
heavy	light	sunshine	rain
severe	strong	showers	wind
thick	thick	thunderstorm	fog

Example: **Thick cloud** on the coast means visibility is less than 100 metres.

1 There has been _____ and some rivers are at danger level.
2 You can expect a few _____ later on, so you may need your umbrella.
3 Today's football is cancelled. They can't see the ball because of the _____ .
4 It's going to be a beautiful weekend with plenty of _____, so don't forget your sun cream.
5 There has been an accident on the highway. A truck has been blown over by the _____ .
6 Skiers have been enjoying yesterday's falls of _____ .
7 Two cars were destroyed by lightning in last night's _____ .

Grammar: reported statements

2 Rewrite the following sentences in direct speech.

Example: She said it had all been a mistake.
'It **was all a mistake**.'

1 He told me that he would invite me to his party.
'I _____ ,'

2 She told me she didn't care what I had done.
'I _____ ,'

3 I told her I'd stayed with Sandra the night before.
'I _____ .'

4 They told me they couldn't come to the meeting the next day.
'We _____ .'

3 Rewrite the following sentences in reported speech.

Example: 'I've been staying in London since yesterday.'
He said **he'd been staying in London since the day before**.

1 'We're very happy with the hotel room.'
They said _____ .

2 'I'll be glad when it's all finished.'
She told me _____ .

3 'You can start the race when I say "Go".'
He told us _____ .

4 'We're going to leave tomorrow.'
They said _____ .

31 Turning points

Vocabulary: things we read

1 Write the letters in the correct order and complete the definitions.

a) bets-relsel   b) zagameni   c) wepssepran   d) lapy
e) volne   f) stewbie   g) yetrop   h) xett ookb

Example: You see it at the theatre: play

1 You can read about fashion and famous people: _____
2 A long, written story about invented people: _____
3 It is often beautiful but hard to understand: _____
4 The writer of this is rich now: _____
5 *Language to go* is one of these: _____
6 A place to find information on the Internet: _____
7 Millions of these are delivered to homes every day: _____

Grammar: past perfect continuous

2 Complete the text about the financier George Soros using the verbs in the box.

a) created   b) had been living   c) had been earning
d) made   e) gave   f) had been working   g) lost
h) moved   i) didn't use   j) moved   k) had

George Soros was born in Budapest in 1930. Before he moved to London in 1947, Soros ¹ _____ in his native country, Hungary, where his father was a lawyer. He later ² _____ another move to the USA. He ³ _____ in the financial centre of London for a number of years, before he ⁴ _____ to New York. In both cities, he speculated on the financial markets and ⁵ _____ huge wealth.

In Wall Street, however, he ⁶ _____ failure as well as success. Up until 1993, his business ⁷ _____ $4,000 a minute! But in 1998, he ⁸ _____ billions of dollars on the currency markets.

Soros became a very rich man but he ⁹ _____ his money only for himself. He ¹⁰ _____ large amounts of money to many schools and colleges around the world.

3 Complete the sentences. Use ONE past simple verb and ONE past perfect continuous verb in each sentence.

1 He _____ (leave) his wife after they _____ (live) together for 35 years.
2 She _____ (miss) the bus because she _____ (look) the wrong way.
3 We _____ (hope) for nice weather for the picnic. But it _____ (rain)!
4 We _____ (stand) for most of the show before we _____ (find) two seats.
5 She _____ (expect) her friend for ages before she finally _____ (arrive).

32 Clean and tidy

Vocabulary: housework and cleanliness

1 Write the letters in the correct order.

Example: Some students don't like homework. (EKHROMOW).

1 I did the _____ (SHOUKROWE) so that the flat is _____ (DYIT) when my parents come for lunch.
2 After the party the house was so _____ (SYEMS) it took hours to clean it.
3 There's a washing machine for the _____ (SINGHAW) and a dishwasher for the _____ . (ISDEHS).
4 Don't forget to _____ (UMUCAV) the carpets and _____ (STUD) the furniture.

Grammar: *have something done* and reflexive pronouns

2 Correct the mistakes in the following sentences. Be careful – not all the sentences are wrong!

Example: I'm not doing the dishes – do it ~~you~~! ✗ *yourself*

1 I shave every morning but today I cut me.
2 She washed herself and went out for dinner.
3 They had a great time. Yes, they really enjoyed.
4 No need to do anything. The lights turn them off at midnight.
5 He bought himself a book of American stories.
6 Do you ever talk to you?

3 Write the words in the correct order.

At a dinner party: G = Guest H = Host

G: The meal is delicious.
   (1) it did have you delivered ?

H: (2) it myself I no actually cooked

G: And I loved the party invitations. So funny!
   (3) them too did make you ?

H: (4) them made had no I .

G: So, come on everybody. Smile for the camera…
   (5) photos the yourself develop you do?

H: Yes, I do.

In a hotel: G = Guest R = Receptionist

G: Can I order a newspaper?

R: Certainly. (6) I sent room one to your shall have?

G: (7) get I No myself can it.
   I also need a wake-up call in the morning.

R: There is a choice here.
   (8) do yourself you it can or can I done it have you for.

G: Perhaps it's best if you do it.

33 Tomorrow's world

Vocabulary: describing changes

1 Find twelve words or expressions to do with change hidden in the word chain. The first has been done for you.

Grammar: future with *will* and *will have done*

2 Match the clauses and use the correct form of the verbs in brackets.

Example: *1-f I hope he will have finished painting that door by tonight.*

1 I hope he *(finish)* painting that door   f
2 By June 14th,   __
3 I have only one more to read   __
4 We *(fly)* for fourteen hours non-stop   __
5 It's their golden wedding tomorrow,   __
6 By 8.30 tonight,   __

a) by the time this flight lands.
b) his train *(reach)* Rome.
c) so they *(be)* married for 50 years.
d) we *(live)* here for ten years.
e) and then I *(read)* all her books.
f) by tonight.

3 Correct the mistakes in the following sentences. Be careful – not all the sentences are wrong!

Example: Will ~~you finished~~ that job by tonight? ✗ *you have finished*

1 By this time next year I will have work here for three years.

2 Most people agree that the future will bring many changes.

3 On January 1st we will be knowing each other for six months.

4 Will you have passed the exam for next July?

5 By the time you read this, I will go to the airport.

6 Will he have received your e-mail yet?

34 Honeymoon horrors

Vocabulary 1: medical problems and symptoms

1 Complete the sentences using the correct form of the word in brackets.

Example: When I was on holiday, I got loads of mosquito *bites*. (bite)

1 My foot feels very _____ . (itch)
2 I was _____ by a snake last year. (bite)

3 Ow! I've been _____ by a bee! (sting)
4 You need to see a doctor – your stomach is very _____ . (swell)
5 Don't get shampoo in your eyes – it really _____ . (sting)
6 What's that _____ on your arm? (swell)
7 My back _____ when I use a computer. (ache)
8 Help! Your dog is _____ mine! (bite)

Vocabulary 2: phrasal verbs about illness

2 Decide which sentences are correct and which are incorrect. Rewrite the incorrect sentences.

Example: He came out in red spots all over his back. ✓ OK

1 He saw the blood and he passed off immediately.
2 He's gone to bed – he doesn't want his headache to turn in something worse.
3 You need a day off work – you're coming down with food poisoning.
4 Oh, what a mess! He's thrown out all over the carpet!
5 It took him a long time to get over the flu.
6 When he eats peanuts, his tongue swells out.
7 It was so hot in the stadium that 30 people passed out.
8 He feels terrible. He thinks he's coming over with something.
9 A fever sometimes makes you come up with a sweat.

35 Ice maiden

Vocabulary: people and groups

1 Complete the sentences using the words in the box.

> family   society   people   team   generation
> culture   status

Example: People who break the law are a danger to
society.

1 His new job gives him higher _____ in the
company.
2 The younger _____ often have different views from
their older relatives.
3 On holiday I go to museums to find out about the
_____ of the country I'm in.
4 The _____ of Poland are always friendly to me.
5 I really hope that our _____ wins today.
6 She's got a big _____ – seven sisters!

Grammar: past modal verbs of deduction

**2 Complete the text about the Nazca lines using the
correct form of the verbs in brackets.**

The Nazca lines

The Nazca lines of Peru are one of the greatest unsolved
mysteries in the world. Historians only discovered these
amazing lines by flying over the desert. _Who could have
made_ (could / make) lines which are only visible from the
air? What [1] _____ (could / be) for?

Many theories have been suggested: the Nazca people
[2] _____ (might / make) a big calendar from the lines.
Others think that the animal designs [3] _____ (might
/ represent) the stars which helped the farmers to plant
food. Some people believe that the lines were art forms
or that the people [4] _____ (could / use) the animal
designs to ask their gods to send rain. The strangest idea
of all is that the lines [5] _____ (might / show) aircraft
from outer space where to land. They are only sure of one
thing: the Nazca people, a civilisation that lived centuries
before the Incas, [6] _____ (must / make) the lines.

**3 Write sentences with _must, might, could, can't_ to
make deductions. Use the words in brackets to help
you.**

Example: He was late for the meeting. (possibly / miss /
train) _He might have missed the train._

1 My wallet was in my bag but now it's gone. (definitely /
lose)
2 I rang the doorbell but nobody answered. (definitely / not
/ hear)
3 They are looking very relaxed and suntanned. (probably /
be / on holiday)
4 The exams were easy but she failed them all. (definitely
/ study / not / enough)
5 I waited for an hour but he didn't come. (maybe / he /
forget)

36 A winning formula

Vocabulary: business processes: word building

**1 Find nine words to do with business. The first has
been done for you.**

M	P	R	O	D	U	C	T	I	O	N
O	R	P	R	O	D	U	C	E	M	P
P	O	L	L	B	M	E	R	I	O	L
E	D	T	R	U	A	K	I	O	S	A
R	U	M	E	S	R	I	P	L	A	N
R	C	O	R	I	K	W	E	N	C	N
A	T	N	A	N	E	U	T	S	E	I
M	A	R	K	E	T	I	N	G	O	N
A	D	V	E	R	T	I	S	E	N	G
P	I	B	U	S	I	N	E	S	S	D

**2 Complete the text below using the words from
Exercise 1. Words can be used more than once.**

How to do business and succeed!

If you believe the [1] _____ for your [2] _____
is growing. It's time to [3] _____ ahead.

To increase your output you'll need to [4] _____
more, but you'll also need your [5] _____ and sales
department to think about how to [6] _____ and sell
your product. At the start of the year [7] _____ costs
will be high and you may need extra money. If this is the
case why not write a [8] _____ _____ and ask
your bank for a loan? Running a [9] _____ needs
careful [10] _____ .

Remember the three Rs: – the **right** [11] _____ in
the **right** place at the **right** time... .

Grammar: non-defining relative clauses

**3 Combine the sentences using a non-defining relative
clause.**

Example: Jakarta is the capital of Indonesia. It is a very
large city.
_Jakarta, which is a very large city, is the capital of
Indonesia._

1 The new marketing director is arriving tomorrow.
His wife works in finance.
2 In my teenage years I used to play sport all day.
I thought life was easy then.
3 New Orleans is in the south of the USA. Jazz is very
popular there.
4 My mother had a lovely birthday party. She is 75 now.
5 The bank manager wants to see me on Monday.
I can never remember his name.
6 My mobile keeps me in touch with the office. I always
have it with me.

37 Old friends

Vocabulary: verb expressions about friendship

1 Underline the correct alternatives.

When I was six, my family <u>moved</u> / lived to Romania for a year. I (1) *started* / *made* friends with a girl of my own age. Now we live in different countries but we (2) *are in touch* / *write news* with each other. It's great to think that over the years I've never (3) *forgotten* / *lost* contact with her. We don't phone very often, so we (4) *keep* / *make* in touch by writing birthday cards. We usually (5) *post* / *send* a lot of news with the cards, so we can (6) *find out* / *keep up* with what has been happening in our lives. I can always (7) *rely with* / *rely on* her to write because she never forgets my birthday. Our friendship is very special and I hope we can (8) *remain* / *continue* friends for another forty years!

Grammar: present perfect with *for* and *since*

2 Put the time expressions in the correct column.

| a) two years   b) ages   c) I arrived   d) Monday |
| e) a week   f) 25th May   g) six months   h) 1999 |
| i) lunch time   j) yesterday   k) this morning |
| l) ten minutes   m) eight o'clock   n) the start of the film |

for	since
a long time	July

3 Write sentences using the present perfect with *for* or *since*. Use the verbs in brackets.

Example: Petra did the course and now she's making her own clothes. **(make)**

Petra's been making her own clothes since she did the course.

1 I'm travelling in Australia. I started last week. **(travel)**
   I _____ .

2 Paulo rode a bicycle until he was 13. Now he's 25. **(not ride)**
   He _____ .

3 Were you here at the beginning of the movie? **(be)**
   Have _____ ?

4 Raul says he's feeling ill. He first felt ill three hours ago. **(feel)**
   Raul _____ .

5 Monika left ages ago. She never calls me. **(not contact)**
   She _____ .

6 Tracey met Brad six months ago. **(know)**
   They _____ .

38 Don't worry, be happy

Vocabulary: happiness

1 Find nine words or expressions to do with happiness and unhappiness. The first has been done for you.

I	N	A	G	O	O	D	M	O	O	D
N	Z	R	L	P	S	E	U	N	A	O
A	B	S	A	T	I	S	F	I	E	D
B	R	A	D	L	E	Y	F	O	P	O
A	R	S	E	N	A	L	Y	A	L	E
D	E	P	R	E	S	S	E	D	E	X
M	I	S	E	R	A	B	L	E	A	T
O	P	T	I	M	I	X	A	N	S	E
O	N	O	T	H	R	I	L	L	E	D
D	E	L	I	G	H	T	E	D	D	Y

Function: polite questions

2 Write the words in the correct order.

Example: worst what telling would is me your fear mind you?
Would you mind telling me what your worst fear is?

1 birthday is would telling me your mind you when?

2 your what is can you ask I weight?

3 much me you earn how could tell you?

4 are you happy know would I if like to

5 drink you me how coffee tell could much you?

6 telling meat you you would me if eat mind?

3 Write indirect questions.

Example: How much do you earn?
Can I ask how much you earn?

1 Are you happy in your work?
   I'd like _____ .

2 What keeps you awake at night?
   Could you _____ ?

3 What do you do in the evenings?
   Would you mind _____ ?

4 How much do you spend on cigarettes?
   Can I _____ ?

5 What makes you depressed?
   Would you mind _____ ?

6 Are you free at the weekend?
   I'd like _____ .

7 Where do you usually go for your holidays?
   Would you mind _____ ?

39 If only …

Vocabulary: shopping

1 Match the words in the box with the definitions below.

> take things back refund buy things on impulse
> browse haggle go window shopping
> try clothes on the sales get a bargain

1 See if trousers, shirts etc. fit: **try clothes on**
2 Spend a long time looking and deciding what to buy: _____
3 Get things from a shop without planning to: _____
4 Time of the year when shops sell things at a discount: _____
5 Return things to the shop: _____
6 Try and pay a cheaper price than they ask: _____
7 Money given back to you for unwanted goods: _____
8 Look at a lot of things without intending to buy them: _____
9 Pay too little for something: _____

Grammar: third conditional and *I wish / if only*

2 Look at the pictures then complete the story using the correct form of the verbs in brackets.

A lucky break!

Last year, Taka and Yoko got married but if it **hadn't been** (be) for a bar of soap they [1] _____ (never meet). Last year Taka had an accident in the shower – he slipped on the soap and broke his leg. He says 'If I [2] _____ (slip) on the soap, I [3] _____ (break) my leg, and if I [4] _____ (break) my leg I [5] _____ (meet) Yoko!' Yoko explains further. 'If I [6] _____ (be) off duty I [7] _____ (look after) Taka when he arrived at the hospital. And if we [8] _____ (meet) we [9] _____ (fall) in love and [10] _____ (get) married!'

3 Write sentences using the third conditional.

Example: I didn't phone my girlfriend on her birthday. (She was upset)
If (only) I'd phoned my girlfriend on her birthday, she wouldn't have been upset.

1 I didn't listen to your advice. (I paid too much)
2 I didn't take a map. (I got lost)
3 She switched her phone off. (She didn't get my message)
4 I didn't travel first class. (I had a terrible flight)
5 I was rude to my boss. (I lost my job)

40 How did it go?

Vocabulary : job applications and interviews

1 Complete the crossword.

1 Certificates, diplomas and degrees are all types of these (14)
2 Plans and aims for your future (4-4,5)
3 and 4 Possibilities for getting better jobs (9,9)
5 Written reports about you and your work from past employers (10)
6 Jobs that you've done in the past (10)
7 Things that you are good at (9)
8 Things that you are not good at (10)
9 A situation when people ask you questions to find out if you should get the job (9)

1	Q	U	A	L	I	F	I	C	A	T	I	O	N	S
2													
3													
4													
5													
6													
7													
8													
9													

Grammar: reported questions

2 Sonia has had an interview for a new job. Read her e-mail and find seven mistakes to do with reported questions. Correct the mistakes – the first has been done for you.

> Niki
>
> I must tell you about my interview. I wasn't at all nervous even though there were three of them there. I think I looked really good in my new suit! First they asked me if ~~am I~~ ✗ I was good with computers and what software have I used. They also wanted to know if can I drive. So that was OK. Then the woman asked me have you any questions.
>
> I asked them am I allowed to smoke in the office. She said I couldn't. Well, I guess I can live with that. :-(
>
> After that, they wanted to know my strengths. I said I was very good with people. They asked if I will can start next month. Finally one of the men wanted to know when can I give them my decision. So that means that I got the job! I'm so happy! :-).
>
> How about you? Did you have a good time with that guy you met? Send me ALL the details! CU L8R!
>
> Sonia

Grammar reference

Lesson 1

Past simple and past continuous

- Use the **past simple** to talk about completed actions or events in the past, often with a time reference (*yesterday, last week, in 1999* etc.):
  *We **met** Tom yesterday.*
  *Julie **didn't speak** to Matthew last week.*
  ***Did** they **go** on holiday last year?*
  *I **visited** my grandmother every Saturday when I was a child.*

- Use the **past continuous** to describe longer actions and events in the past:
  *I **was lying** awake at three o'clock last night.*

- Use the **past continuous** to set the scene in a story:
  *The rain **was falling** and the wind **was blowing** through the trees in the dark forest …*

- Use the **past simple** and **past continuous** together in one sentence if the first action is still going on when the second action happens:
  *He **was driving** his car very fast when a dog **ran** in front of him.*

Lesson 2

Subject and object questions

Subject question	Object question
***Who** saw Vic? (Marjorie) (who is the **subject** of the question)*	***Who** did Marjorie see? (Vic) (who is the **object** of the question)*

- When a **wh-** word is the subject of the sentence, it comes before the verb. We do not use the auxiliary *do* or *did*, we use a main verb in the correct tense:
  Who ate my cake?
  NOT ~~Who did eat my cake?~~
  What's happened? The flat is a mess!
  NOT ~~What did happen?~~

- When a **wh-** word is the object, normal question word order with an auxiliary is used:
  ***Who** is David talking to? Jan.*
  ***What** did the teacher say to the students? She told them to open their books.*

Lesson 3

The future with *will* and *going to*

- Use *will* to make a decision at the time of speaking:
  I've got a terrible headache.   Have you? I'll get you some aspirins.
  The film's at four.   Great! I'll come with you.

- Use *will* with the expressions *I think* and *I don't think*:
  *Do you want to come to the party? Yes, I think I **will**.*
  I think I'll go to bed now.   OK. See you in the morning.
  I don't think I'll call the dog 'Bones'. It sounds too silly.
  NOT ~~I think I won't call~~ … OR ~~I don't think I won't call~~…

- Use *going to* to talk about decisions you have made for the future, before the moment of speaking:
  *I'm **going to** call the baby James.*
  *We're **going to** spend a week in France.*

Lesson 4

Comparatives and superlatives

- Use the **comparative** form of adjectives with *than* to compare two things:
  *Retraining is **harder** for him **than** it is for me.*
  NOT ~~Retraining is more harder for him~~…
  OR ~~Retraining is as harder for him~~…

- Use adjectives with *(not) as … as* to compare two things:
  *I'm **as tall as** you. (We're the same height.)*
  *This house **isn't as big as** the other one. (This house is smaller.)*

- Use the **superlative** form of adjectives to compare three or more things:
  *He was **the oldest** lecturer at the college.*

Spelling rule	Adjective	Comparative	Superlative
One syllable ending in a vowel: add -r / -st	large	larger	largest
One syllable ending in a consonant: add -er / -est	cheap	cheaper	cheapest
One syllable ending in consonant + vowel + consonant: **double the consonant** and add -er / -est	fat	fatter	fattest
Two syllables ending in **y**: **change y to i** + -est	heavy	heavier	heaviest
Two or more syllables: add **more** or **most**	beautiful	more beautiful	most beautiful
Irregular adjectives	bad good	worse better	worst best

Lesson 5

Modal verbs for ability

- Use *can* to talk about ability in the present:
  *I **can** write with both hands.*
  *You **can't** swim.*
  ***Can** Jane speak Italian?*

- Use *could* to talk about ability in the past:
  *I **could** read when I was four.*
  *Sam **couldn't** write until he was five.*
  ***Could** you run fast when you were a child?*

- Use *was able to* or *managed to* to talk about something that was possible on one particular occasion in the past:
  *It took a long time, but we **were able to** fix the car in the end.*
  *I **managed to** escape through the window.*

- Use *wasn't able to, didn't manage to* or *couldn't* to talk about something that was not possible on a particular occasion in the past:
  *Unfortunately, we **weren't able to** fix the car.*
  *I **didn't manage to** escape. I had to be rescued.*
  *They **couldn't** find the exit.*

Lesson 6

Expressing purpose

- Use **adverbs of purpose** (*to, in order to, so as to, so that* etc.) to give reasons for an action:
  *Security companies are installing cameras **in order to** watch employees.*
  *Software is used **so that** they can record the websites you visit.*

Lesson 7

Present perfect simple vs past simple

- Use the **present perfect** to talk about past experiences. It is not important when the experiences happened:
  *I**'ve worked** as a manager and a supervisor. (At some time – it isn't important when.)*
  ***Have** you ever **visited** the Acropolis in Athens? (At any time in your life?)*
  *I**'ve never tasted** oysters – are they nice? (Never in my life.)*

- Use the **past simple** to talk about completed actions in the past, often with a time reference (*yesterday, last week, in July* etc.):
  *I **applied** for the job in 2001.*
  *We **ate** fish at the restaurant yesterday.*
  ***Did** they **go** to Rome last year?*

Lesson 8

Managing a conversation – verb patterns

- Note the following verb patterns:

Pleased + to + infinitive	I'm pleased to be here.
Lovely + to + infinitive	It's lovely to see you again.
Congratulate + somebody + on	I congratulated Isabelle on her exam success.
Congratulations + on	Congratulations on your recent engagement.
Send + something + to	Please send my love to your parents.
Introduce + somebody + to	David introduced me to his mother.

Lesson 9

First conditional

- The form of the first conditional is:
  If + **present simple + modal verb + infinitive**

- Use the **first conditional** to talk about future possibilities:
  *If you **use** sun cream, you **won't get** sunburn.*
  ***You'll get** wet if you **don't take** rain clothes.*
  ***Will** I **need** rain clothes **if** I **go** in June?*

- Use the **first conditional** to make suggestions, give advice or warnings:
  If you plan several flights, it'll be cheaper to buy a pass.
  If you book your ticket well in advance, you'll get a better price.
  If you don't like hot weather, go in December.

- You can also use **imperatives** in first conditional sentences:
  *If you're going out, **take** the dog with you.*

- ***Unless*** means *if not*:
  *Don't go to Australia **unless** you like hot weather.*
  (Don't go to Australia **if** you **don't** like hot weather.)

> Note: The *if* clause often comes first but it can come second:
> *If you use sun cream, you won't get sunburn.*
> *You won't get sunburn if you use sun cream.*
> When the *if* clause comes first, put a comma after it. You don't need a comma when it comes second.

Lesson 10

Verb constructions for likes and dislikes

- Use the *-ing* form or a **noun** after these verbs: *like, love, enjoy, hate, don't mind, can't stand*:
  *I love **playing** basketball.*
  *I can't stand **junk food**.*

- Use the **infinitive** with *to* after these verbs: *want, decide, need, forget, learn, promise, would like / love / hate*:
  *I want **to take** more exercise.*
  *I'd love **to play** baseball.*

- Use the *-ing* form or a **noun** after a preposition:
  *I'm sick of **running** round the park.*
  *I'm keen on **aerobics**.*

- Use the **infinitive** after modal verbs (*can, will, should, must* etc.):
  *I must **go** out.*
  *We can **play** tennis tomorrow.*

Lesson 11

Used to and *would*

- Use *used to* + **infinitive** for repeated actions in the past that don't happen now:
  *I **used to drink** a lot of coffee.* (But now I don't.)
  *Women **didn't use to smoke** in public.*
  (But now they do.)
  ***Did** Harry **use to smoke**?*

- Use *used to* to talk about past states:
  *Sarah **used to** have long hair.*

- Use *would* to talk about repeated actions in the past:
  *We **would** spend our holidays by the sea.*
  *My grandfather **would** sit in his chair and tell us stories.*

Lesson 12

Verbs with two objects

- Verbs can have one object or two. They can have a **direct object**:
  *I sent **a letter**.*

- And an **indirect object**:
  *I sent a letter **to you**.*

- The **indirect object** is often a person, and often goes before the **direct object**:
  *I sent <u>you</u> **a letter**.*
  *We offer <u>you</u> **a first-class service**.*

- Sometimes the **indirect object** goes after the **direct object**. When this happens, there is usually a preposition:
  *We can lend **money** to <u>you</u>.*

Lesson 13

Present simple and continuous for future

- Use the **present simple** to talk about timetables and programmes in the future:
  ***Does** the boat **leave** at six this evening?*
  *The tour **starts** at 7.30 tomorrow.*
  *The film **doesn't finish** at eight, it **finishes** at half past eight.*

> Note: You often see this use of the **present simple** in organisations or institutions, e.g. schools, offices, shops etc.

- Use the **present continuous** and a time reference (*tomorrow, next week, at ten o'clock*, etc.) to talk about definite future arrangements you have made yourself:
  *I'm **seeing** the doctor at four o'clock.*
  *We're **travelling** to Lisbon next Saturday.*

Lesson 14

Phrasal verbs

- A phrasal verb is a **verb** and a **particle**, like *out, on,* or *over,* which has a different meaning from the verb on its own. There are four kinds of phrasal verbs:

1 Phrasal verbs can be **intransitive** (no object needed):
*We **set off** at 9.00.* NOT ~~We set off the journey at 9.00.~~

2 Or **transitive** (they need an object):
*He **got over** the death of his father.* NOT ~~He got over.~~

3 Some **transitive** phrasal verbs are **separable** (the verb and the particle can be separated by the object):
*I **put** Ewa **up** for the night.*
*I **put up** Ewa for the night.*

If the object is a pronoun, the verb and the particle must be separated:
*I **put** her **up** for the night.* NOT ~~I put up her for the night.~~

Some **transitive** phrasal verbs are **not** separable (the verb and particle cannot be separated):
*Can you **look after** the baby?*
*Can you **look after** her?*
NOT ~~Can you look the baby after?~~
OR ~~Can you look her after?~~

4 Some **transitive** phrasal verbs have **two particles** which are not separable:
*Students usually **look up to** their teachers.*
NOT ~~Students usually look their teachers up to.~~

Lesson 15

Modal verbs for giving advice

- Use *should, could* or *ought to* to give advice:
*You **should** get more sleep.*
*You **shouldn't** work so hard*
*You **could** try going to bed earlier.*
*You **ought to** do more exercise during the day*

- Use the **infinitive** without *to* after modal verbs:
*You **should** take more exercise.*
NOT ~~You should to take~~ …

Lesson 16

Defining relative clauses

- Use **relative pronouns** (*who, which, that, where, whose*) to introduce **relative clauses**:
*Lavender has a smell **that** calms people down.*

- Use *who* or *that* for people, *which* or *that* for things, *where* for places, *when* for times and *whose* for people and their possessions:
*Jane's the girl **who** told me to buy some lavender oil.*
*Lemon has a smell **which** increases people's energy.*
*This is the village **where** my husband grew up.*
*I like nighttime **when** the town is nice and quiet.*
*That's the man **whose** house we stayed in last summer.*

- Use **relative clauses** to define the person or thing you are talking about:
That's the man.
*That's the man **who bought my house.***
(The relative clause defines 'the man'.)

> Note: You don't need a relative pronoun when you are defining the object of a sentence: *Cherries are the fruit (that) I like most.*

Lesson 17

Present perfect simple with *yet, already, just*

- Use the **present perfect** to talk about actions that happened in the past and have an effect on the present:
*My neighbour **has** just **painted** his front door.* (It looks good now.)
*Kim **has** already **written** her report.* (The report is finished now.)

- Use *already* when the action is completed:
*I've **already** tidied my desk.* (My desk is tidy now.)

- Use *just* when the action happened very recently:
*I've **just** repainted my bedroom.* (I finished painting a few moments ago.)

- *Already* and *just* come before the verb:
*She's **already** bought some plants.*
*He's **just** tidied the house.*

- *Yet* comes at the end of the sentence.
*I haven't walked the dog **yet**.*

- Use *not yet* when the action is not completed but you expect it to be completed in the future.
*I haven't bought a fish tank **yet**.* (But I will soon.)
*George hasn't finished that book **yet**.* (But he'll finish it in the next week.)

- Use *yet* to ask whether an action is completed:
*Have you taken up a sport **yet**?* (Are you doing a new sport now?)

> Note: *Already* can also go at the end of a sentence for emphasis:
Have you prepared the food already? (You did that quickly.)

Lesson 18

Informal and polite requests

Asking someone to do something	Saying 'yes'	Saying 'no'
Open the window!	OK.	
Can you open the window?	Yes, of course.	Sorry, I can't reach it.
Could you open the window?	Sure.	
Do you mind opening the window?	Not at all.	Yes, I do – it's cold in here.
Would you mind opening the window?	No, of course not.	Actually, I would mind.

Asking permission to do something	Saying 'yes'	Saying 'no'
Can I open the window?	Yes, of course.	I'd rather you didn't.
Could I open the window?	Sure.	
Do you mind if I open the window?	Not at all.	Yes, I do – it's cold in here.
Would you mind if I opened the window?	No, of course not.	Actually, I would mind.

Lesson 19

Second conditional

- The form of the second conditional is:
  If + past simple, *would* (or *could* or *might*) + infinitive

- Use the **second conditional** to talk about unlikely or imaginary situations in the present and the future:
  *If I **didn't have** a car, I'd **take** the train.*
  (But I have got a car, so I won't take the train.)
  *If I **won** the race, I'd **be** delighted.*
  (But I probably won't win the race so I won't be delighted.)
  ***Would** you **stop** working if you **won** the lottery?*
  (You probably won't win the lottery.)

Note: You can use *were* or *was* with *I, he, she* and *it*:
*If I **were** rich, I'd buy a house abroad.*
*If she **were** taller, she could be a model.*
*If it **wasn't** raining, we'd go to the beach.*

Note: The *if* clause often comes first but it can come second:
If I were richer, I'd be happier.
I'd be happier if I were richer.
When the *if* clause comes first, put a comma after it. You don't need a comma when it comes second.

Lesson 20

Verb constructions with *-ing* / infinitive

- Use the **infinitive** with *to* after these verbs: **want, decide, need, learn, promise, would like / love / hate, plan, afford, manage, offer**:
  *I **want to go** out tonight.*
  *Do you **need to buy** some new jeans?*
  *He didn't **promise to write** but I'm sure he will.*

Note: You can also use **verb + object + infinitive** with *to* after the verbs *want* and *would like / love / hate*:
*I'd **love you to come** on holiday with me.*
*They **wanted her to join** the swimming club.*

- Use the **-ing form** after these verbs: **like, enjoy, love, hate, finish, go, stop, avoid, spend / waste time** and after some two-part phrasal verbs: **give up, take up, carry on, keep on**:
  *I **avoid taking** exercise.*
  *He **keeps on laughing** at her.*
  *Do you **avoid writing** letters?*
  *I **don't waste time surfing** the Internet.*

Lesson 21

Past perfect simple

- Use the **past perfect** to talk about an action that happened before another action in the past:
  *When I arrived at the terminal, the plane **had already taken off**.*
  (First the plane took off, then I arrived at the terminal.)
  *I realised I **hadn't packed** my passport.*
  (First I left my passport behind, then I realised.)
  ***Had** the meeting **started** when you arrived?*

Note: The difference between the **past perfect** and the **past simple** is:
*When I **arrived** at the bus stop, the bus left.*
(I arrived and the bus left at the same time.)
*When I **arrived** at the bus stop, the bus had left.*
(The bus left, then I arrived.)

Lesson 22

Passive constructions

- Use the **passive** when you don't know who does the action, or you are not interested in who does it, or it isn't important who does it:
  *The winner of the competition **was announced** during the show.*
  (It isn't important who announced the winner.)

- Use the **passive** to talk about processes:
  *First the band **is chosen**. Then a single **is released**. Next, a full-length album **is recorded** …*

- Use the **passive** in more formal contexts:
  *The new president **was taken** to the White House where he **was interviewed** by a senior journalist …*

- Use **by** + **agent** (the person or thing) when we want to say who did the action.
  *… he was interviewed **by a senior journalist**.
  The film was directed **by Almodóvar**.*

  > Note: The **object** of an active sentence becomes the **subject** of the passive sentence:
  > *People broadcast **the programmes**.*   (Active)
  > ***The programmes** are broadcast.*   (Passive)

- Use the verb **be** in the correct tense + **past participle**:
  *The Spice Girls **were created** by a businessman.
  The bridge **is being built** at the moment.
  This room **has been painted** recently.*

Lesson 23

Modal verbs to talk about future probability

- Use **will** to talk about things that you think are very likely to happen in the future:
  *I'm sure interactive books **will** become very popular.
  We **won't** live on other planets.
  Will we use cars?*

- Use **may, might** or **could** to talk about possibilities in the future:
  *I think we **may** communicate entirely by e-mail.
  We **might not** need telephones at all.
  Robots **could** be in every home in fifty years.*

Lesson 24

Phrasal verbs – see Lesson 14

Lesson 25

Modal verbs for necessity and obligation

- Use *I must* and *I mustn't* to talk about your own obligations:
  *I **must** keep my writing simple.* (This is what I feel is necessary.)
  *I **mustn't** forget Andy's birthday.* (I am reminding myself to do something.)

- Use *have to* or *must* to talk about obligations that come from other people:
  *You **have to** send that e-mail today.* (The boss says it's necessary.)
  *I **have to** be at the office by eight o'clock.* (These are the company rules.)
  *You **mustn't** park here.* (It's the law.)

  > Note: The usual question form is *Do I have to …?* not ~~Must I?~~
  > *Do I have to retype this report?*
  > *Do we have to leave so early?*

- Use *don't have to* when something is unnecessary:
  *You **don't have to** use abbreviations in e-mails.* (It isn't necessary.)

- Use *should* and *shouldn't* to ask for and give advice. Use *should* to say something is a good idea, and *shouldn't* to say it's a bad idea.
  *You **should** get more fresh air.
  You **shouldn't** smoke.*

Lesson 26

Ways to express contrasting ideas

- Use *although, despite (not), in spite of* and *however* to introduce contrasting ideas:
  *Sasha didn't phone Peter, **although** she'd planned to.
  Despite going to bed very late, we all got up at six.
  Did you enjoy your holiday **in spite of** the terrible weather?*

- Note the different forms:
  although + clause
  ***Although** I hate commuting, I love my job.*

  despite (not) + *-ing* form
  ***Despite** leaving at six, I arrived late.
  Despite not having an alarm clock, I manage to wake up early.*

  in spite of + noun or *-ing* form
  ***In spite of** his health, he climbed the mountain.
  He climbed the mountain, **in spite of being** in bad health.*

  However + clause (*However* goes at the start of a sentence.)
  *I often feel tired. **However**, I enjoy the job.*

Lesson 27

Present perfect simple and continuous

- Use both the **present perfect simple** and the **present perfect continuous** to talk about recent actions and situations that have a result in the present.

- Use the **present perfect simple** when you focus on the *result* of a completed activity:
  He's tested the power device and it works.
  I haven't revised for my exam – I think I'll fail.
  Have you run a marathon?

- Use the **present perfect continuous** when you focus on the *activity*. The activity may or may not be completed:
  He's been testing the power device.
  I haven't been revising, I've been sleeping!
  Have you been running?

Lesson 28

Past obligation and permission

- Use *had to / didn't have to* or *made / didn't make* to talk about obligation in the past:

  He had to go to school every day.
  (Someone obliged him to do this.)

  Mum made Peter work in silence.
  (Someone obliged him to work in silence.)

  Did he have to wear a uniform?
  (Was it necessary?)

  They didn't make him work very hard.
  (No one obliged him to work hard.)

- Use *let / didn't let* or *was(n't)/were(n't) / allowed* to say that something was or wasn't permitted:

  Mum often let him watch TV.
  (She gave him permission this.)

  She was allowed to go to the disco
  (Someone gave her permission to do this.)

  Did she let him eat chocolate?
  (Did she give him permission to eat it?)

  Was he allowed to stay up late?
  (Did someone give him permission to do this?)

  She didn't let him go to discos.
  (She refused him permission to do this.)

  He wasn't allowed to eat sweets.
  (Someone refused him permission to do this.)

Lesson 29

First and second conditional
(See also Lessons 9 and 19)

- Use the **first conditional** to talk about things that may or may not happen in the future:
  If you have a business lunch, it'll only last an hour.
  (You may or may not have a business lunch.)
  If it's sunny tomorrow, I'll go out.
  (It's possible that it'll be sunny.)

- Use the **second conditional** to talk about imaginary situations in the present and the future:
  If I wasn't at a meeting, I'd be at home.
  (But I am at a meeting, so I'm not at home.)
  If someone offered me a bribe, I'd probably take it.
  (But I probably won't be offered a bribe.)

Lesson 30

Reported statements

- You can start reported speech in two ways:

1 **Subject + *told* + object (+ *that*)**
  I told him that I was ready to go.

2 **Subject + *said* (+ *that*)**
  I said that I was ready to go.

- When you report what somebody said, the verb tenses usually move back:

  I'm ready to go.

  He said that he was ready to go.

  We went to the market.

  They said they'd been to the market.

  I've been to Aberdeen.

  She said she'd been to Aberdeen.

  Note: There is no change with the past perfect:
  'Mark had arrived late, as usual.' → *He said Mark had arrived late as usual.*

- The time expressions (*yesterday, this week* etc.) also usually change:

> I saw John **yesterday**.

*She said that she had seen John **the day before**.*

> I'm going to work **tomorrow**.

*He told me he was going to work **the following day**.*

> The film is coming out **this week**.

*They said that the film was coming out **that week**.*

> **Note:** After *say* and *tell* + object, you don't need *that*.
> Peter **said that** he was hungry. OR Peter **said** he was hungry.
> Peter **told me that** he was hungry. OR Peter **told me** he was hungry.

Lesson 31

Past perfect simple and continuous
(See also Lesson 21)

- Use the **past perfect simple** to talk about an action that happened before another action in the past:
*When she returned to the UK, she **had already written** some of Harry Potter.*
(First she wrote some of her book, then she returned to the UK.)

- Use the **past perfect continuous** to talk about longer activities or situations that happened before another action in the past:
*Before 1996, Joanne **had been living** in Portugal.*
(Up to 1996, Joanne was living in Portugal.)
*I'd **been waiting** for ages before I was served.*
*They **hadn't been expecting** Mario to arrive so late.*
***Had** they **been seeing** each other long when they got married?*

Lesson 32

Reflexive pronouns

- Use reflexive pronouns (*myself, yourself, ourselves* etc.) to make the subject of the sentence stronger:
*I do everything **myself**.* (Nobody helps me.)
*When Peter was little, he never did anything **himself**. His mother did it all.*
*Don't worry about food for tonight. We'll cook it **ourselves**.*
*Can the twins dress **themselves** yet or are they still too young?*

- Use the structure *have + something + past participle* (also known as the causative) to say that somebody does something for you:
*I **have my hair cut** once a month.*
(Somebody cuts it for me. I don't cut it.)

- If you want to say who does the action for you, use **by + person / thing**:
*I have my car serviced **by Olds Motor Group**.*
*John has his hair cut **by a friend**.*

- Form: Use the correct tense of *have + something + past participle*:
*I **have my bike repaired** at 'Wheelies'.*
*I'm going to **have this room painted**.*

Lesson 33

The future

- Use *will / won't* + infinitive to say what you think will happen at a point in the future:
*I think we **will** all **wear** personal computers on our wrists.*

- Use *will / won't* + *have* + past participle to say that you think something will happen before or at a point in the future:

*By 2050, scientists **will have perfected** the 'brainlink' computer.*

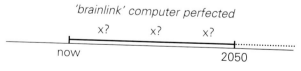

*This time next week, I **will have been** on holiday for two days.*

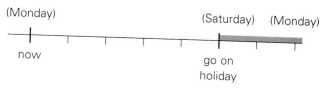

Lesson 34

Phrasal verbs – see Lesson 14

Lesson 35

Past modal verbs of deduction

- Use *must have been* when you are sure something was true:
  She must have been a storyteller.
  (I am sure she was a storyteller.)

- Use *can't have been* when you are sure something wasn't true:
  She can't have been an ordinary member of society.
  (I am sure she wasn't an ordinary member of society.)

- Use *might have been* or *could have been* when you think something was possible:
  I think she might have been a soldier.
  She could have been a rich and powerful woman.

  Note: We can also make deductions about things in the present.

- Use **must be** when you are sure something is true:
  That must be an insect – it's got six legs.

- Use **can't be** when you are sure something isn't true:
  That can't be a spider. It's only got six legs. Spiders have got eight legs.

- Use **might be** when you think something is possible:
  I think it might be a bee.

Lesson 36

Non-defining relative clauses

- Use non-defining relative clauses to add extra information to a sentence:
  My car is two years old.
  My car, which needs a service, is two years old.

  My pet rabbit died in June last year.
  My pet rabbit, who was adorable, died in June last year.

- Introduce non-defining relative clauses with *who* or *which*, not ~~that~~:
  Kate Moss, who is an international model, bought one of the T-shirts.
  Arezzo, which isn't very far from Siena, is an interesting town.

  Note: Use commas before and after non-defining relative clauses.

Lesson 37

Present perfect with *for* and *since*

- Use the **present perfect** with *for* and *since* to talk about actions or states that started in the past and continue now:
  I've known Richard for five years.
  (We met five years ago and I still know him now.)
  I've been living with my brother since I sold my flat.
  (And I'm still living with him.)

  Note: There are many situations when either form is correct.
  I've worked in London for five years.
  I've been working in London for five years.

- The **present perfect continuous** is often used when we talk about something temporary:
  I've been taking the bus to work recently.
  (My car isn't working.)

  Note: The following verbs are not normally used in the continuous form: *know, have, like, enjoy, hate, love, want, need, believe, understand.*

- Use *for* to talk about the length of time:
  for eight days   for months   for a long time

- Use *since* to say when the action or state started:
  since three o'clock   since last Tuesday   since 2000

Lesson 38

Polite or indirect questions

- You can ask polite (or indirect) questions with *Could you, Can you, Would you* and *I'd like ...* . If you use a question word, the question word (*when, where, why, what, who* and *how*) goes before the subject:
  Could you tell me when the film starts?
  Would you find out why Sarah looks so upset, please?

- Use *if* or *whether* when the direct question is a yes / no question:
  Can you tell me if you'd like to have dinner sometime?
  I'd like to know whether you want to go out tomorrow.

Lesson 39

Third conditional and *I wish / If only*

- The form of the **third conditional** is:
  If + had / hadn't + past participle, *would / wouldn't* + have + past participle

- Use the **third conditional** to talk about how things might have been different in the past. Third conditional sentences can express relief, regret and accusations:
  *If they **hadn't phoned** us, they **wouldn't have found** out we needed help.*
  (But they did phone, and they did find out.)
  *If I **hadn't worn** the hat, I **wouldn't have felt** so stupid.*
  (But I did wear the hat, and I did feel stupid.)
  *If you **hadn't told** Jane you'd broken her vase, she'd **never have noticed**!*
  (But you did tell her, and she did notice.)

- You can also use *I wish I had / hadn't* + past participle and *If only I had / hadn't* + past participle:
  I wish I had gone to bed earlier! (But I didn't.)
  If only I hadn't gone to bed so late! (But I did.)

> **Note:** The *if* clause often comes first but it can come second:
> If I hadn't been so late, I'd have seen the movie.
> I'd have seen the movie if I hadn't been so late.
> When the *if* clause comes first, put a comma after it. You don't need a comma when it comes second.

Lesson 40

Reported questions

- When you report questions that others have asked, the two types of questions are reported in different ways:

1 **Questions that start with a question word (*who, what, where* etc.):**

   Person + *asked (me)* + question word + subject + (modal verb) + main verb

> What are your strengths?

She asked me what my strengths were.
NOT ... ~~what were my strengths~~.

> What would you do in a crisis?

She asked me what I would do in a crisis.
NOT ... ~~what would I do in a crisis~~.

> Why do you want the job?

She asked me why I wanted the job.
NOT ... ~~why did I want the job~~.

2 **Yes / No questions:**

   Person + *asked (me)* + *if* or *whether* + subject + (modal verb) + main verb

> Can you work under pressure?

He asked if I could work under pressure.

> Are you interested in the job?

He wanted to know whether I was interested in the job.

- When you report questions, the verb tenses usually move back:

> Do you **like** office life?

*She asked if I **liked** office life.*

> **Note:** For more information about changes of tense in reported speech, see pages 114 – 115.

Recording scripts

Lesson 1 It's absolutely true!

Exercise 4

1 A: Were you very hot?
   B: Hot? I was absolutely boiling!
2 A: Were you really tired?
   B: Yes, I was absolutely exhausted!
3 A: Was it very crowded?
   B: Yes, it was really packed!
4 A: Was the stadium very big?
   B: Big? It was absolutely enormous!
5 A: Was the music good?
   B: Good? It was absolutely fantastic!

Exercise 5

S = Sara   R = Rob

R: So, where were you staying?
S: In Brazil, in Rio.
R: Oh, nice one!
S: ... and it was before Carnival – Tuesday I think – yes, Tuesday and, well, you know what Brazil is like in February?
R: Very hot, I imagine?
S: Hot! It's absolutely boiling!
R: Mmmm
S: Well usually.
R: Right.
S: But this year it was raining – heavy rain – something like a metre of water an hour. I'm not exaggerating!! It was very, very wet – in fact, the Sambadrome was absolutely flooded!
R: What's the Sambadrome?
S: Oh you know, it's where they do the Samba. And everyone was getting very worried in case they cancelled the Carnival or something.
R: That would have been really awful.
S: Yes. Just imagine the hundreds and thousands of people involved in the Carnival, and the 200,000 tourists or so, all waiting and then it's cancelled!
R: Incredible!
S: But then the weather changed, and the rain stopped
R: That was lucky.
S: Yeah, so the Carnival started on time after all, and the schools did their Samba – it was so colourful. Did you know there are over 70,000 dancers?
R: Must have been very crowded?
S: Not just crowded – really, really packed!!
R: Mmmm
S: ... and so I went and danced all night, and all the next night.
R: I guess you were tired?
S: Exhausted! But I didn't mind ...
R: No?
S: ... because I was in Brazil ... and it was Carnival.
R: Right.
S: Absolutely fantastic! Absolutely fantastic! Anyway, what about you? Where did you go?
R: Me? Oh, I went to Brighton for a week with my mother. It rained every day.

Lesson 3 What's in a name?

Exercise 4

1 M = Man   W = Woman

M: We really need to choose a name. We're at the hospital, the baby's coming and we still haven't got one! What do you think?
W: Just open the book then and we'll take the first name we find.
M: Are you sure?
W: Yes! Just do it!
M: OK, here goes, I hope we'll like it ... it's ... ur ... STANLEY ... that's it, that's the name. We're going to call our baby boy Stanley. I hope it suits him.
W: Mmm Stanley ... Stan Thornton. I like that. I'm sure it'll suit him.

2 M = Man   W = Woman

M: Darling, she's beautiful. Ah, well done, I'm so proud of you.
W: Isn't she a miracle? Such tiny hands! What are we going to call her though?
M: I dunno ... look it's getting light ... what a beautiful sunrise.
W: That's it! That's the name.
M: What 'Sunrise'?
W: No silly! Dawn! Let's call her Dawn.
M: Yeah. I'll go for that! Welcome to the world baby Dawn!

3 W = Woman   J = John

W: John, we've talked about this so many times. I really want to decide so I can stop worrying about it, OK? It's either Lulu, Lily or Lola.
J: OK, OK! Well, Lulu's the name of a famous singer, so I don't think I'll call her that – it's not very original. As for Lily, it reminds me of a flower! But Lola has a strong image. Let's choose Lola.
W: Yeah, you're right. Lola does sound good.
J: That's it then. Our baby's going to be called Lola.

4 M = Man   W = Woman

M: We'd already decided to name the baby Sammy. That way we covered both sexes.
W: Yeah that's right. But we never expected to have to find another name. When we found out there were two of them, it was such a shock.
M: You can say that again! Twins!
W: Of course we needed another name. So instead of Sammy, we finally decided to use my grandparents' names.
M: Yes. We're going to name the twins Matilda and George.

5 W = Woman   M = Man

W: Now I understand why you like the name Kevin! It's that footballer isn't it?
M: Umm yeah.
W: I'm not going to call my baby after a footballer!
M: But it's a good name.
W: Well, maybe I'll agree to it, if I can give him his second name. I want something a bit more stylish, you know, like a film star.
M: Eh? Oh, all right then.
W: Yeah ... Kevin ... Leonardo ... Jones.

Exercise 7

1 I'll go for that!
2 Maybe we'll use a name book
3 We're going to call her Georgia.
4 Are you definitely going to move to Boston.
5 I'm not sure I'm going to like it.

Lesson 4 Career paths

Exercise 6

A Re-training is harder for me than it is for younger people.
B Studying is more important than working.
C He was the oldest lecturer.
D It was the most boring thing I ever did.
E I was the most experienced lecturer.

Lesson 5 On the other hand

Exercise 1

A: Easy.
B: It was a piece of cake.
   I found it no trouble.
   It was simple.
   It was straightforward.

A: OK.
B: I found it manageable.
   It was possible.

A: Difficult.
B: It was hard.
   It was tough.
   I found it complicated.
   It was impossible.

Exercise 4

M = Mike   J = Joanna

M: I didn't realise you were left-handed.
J: Why do you ask? Are you left-handed too?
M: Yeah. Well, actually I'm a bit ambidextrous 'cos I write with my left hand and I draw with my left hand but ...
J: Yes – I've heard a lot of artists are left-handed.
M: Yeah ... but for sports and things I usually use my right hand. You know, things like I bat right-handed and ...
J: Oh really? I know what you mean, 'cos um, I use my right hand to serve in tennis, but then I change the racket to my left to carry on playing!
M: Yeah and I kick a ball with my right foot instead of my left foot. I suppose that makes me right-footed! Hey! Do you want to try this test I read about – it's a kind of ability test to see if you're ambidextrous? I don't think it'll take long.
J: Oh, OK then, what do you have to do?

Exercise 5

M: So, let's check our results. I managed to throw the ball OK. In fact, it was quite easy with either hand.
J: Yeah, me too – it was a piece of cake. How about the writing though? Huh, look at my message, I couldn't do that at all – it looks like a five-year-old did it!
M: Hmm you're right! You know I actually found it hard at first, but then it wasn't too difficult.
J: Yeah it's not bad at all – I can read it OK. What about the scissors? I found I could use them better with my right hand than I could with my left.
M: Yeah me too. It felt more straightforward with my right hand.
J: So, that leaves the drawing! Let's have a look at yours. Oh, it's really good!
M: Thanks!
J: I wasn't able to hold my pencil properly!
M: Hmm, I can see that. Is that supposed to be me?!

Lesson 7 Teamwork

Exercise 3

I = Interviewer   D = Dan

I: So, Mr Gray, thank you for coming to talk to us today. I'd like to start off with some questions …
D: OK. Fine.
I: … about your experience.
D: Right. Go ahead.
I: Have you had a job like this before?
D: Not exactly.
I: Oh. Have you worked in an office?
D: Pardon?
I: I mean, for example, have you ever used a computer?
D: Well, you see … er … no, I haven't.
I: All right … then what about events? Have you organised an event?
D: … er yes … sort of … er, no.
I: Mmmm. Mr Gray, you've applied for this job …
D: … yep …
I: … and I want to know about your work experience.
D: Yeah … and I'm trying to tell you.
I: I mean, have you ever worked in a team?
D: Team? Oh yeah … Yeah, yeah. Yes, I have.
I: Good, good. Now that is important. When did you do that?
D: Well, all the time – with the team.
I: The team?
D: Yeah, I work for a basketball club …

Exercise 7

1 Have you had a job like this before?
2 Have you worked in an office?
3 Have you ever used a computer?
4 No, I haven't.
5 Have you organised an event?
6 You've applied for this job.
7 Have you ever worked in a team?
8 Yes, I have.

Lesson 8 Nice to meet you

Exercise 3

B = Barry   S = Susie   T = Tom

B: Susie?! Hi! What a nice surprise. I didn't expect to see you here!
S: Hey! Barry! It's great to see you! I can't believe this! What are you doing here?
B: I'm on holiday! How about you? You know, I haven't seen you since you left the UK! How are you getting on?
S: Great! In fact, I'm very well … what about you?
B: I'm fine, thanks.
S: Um … Can I introduce you? Barry, this is my boyfriend, Tom … Tom this is Barry. We met in England.
B: Pleased to meet you, Tom.
T: Nice to meet you, too, Barry.

Exercise 4

S: Tom, did I tell you that Barry's from Wales – he's Welsh.
T: Really? How interesting, and how do you like the States?
B: It's great! I just love the weather here. I'm really enjoying the sunshine.
T: Hey, better than your awful British summers, huh? When I was in London, it rained the whole time!

B: Yes, well … anyway. Susie, you look very well, and I love the new hair style.
S: Do you? Thank you.
B: No, it really, really suits you! You look better every time I see you.
S: Thank you. By the way, did you hear that I'm doing a Masters degree?
B: A Masters? No. What in?
S: Information Technology.
B: That's brilliant! Well done.
S: Oh, is that the time!? Look, I'm real sorry – we've got to go, I'm afraid. We're meeting my Mom, and she gets worried if I'm late.
B: Well, good to see you again Suz, and um … it was good to meet you, um … Todd.
T: Actually, it's Tom.
B: Sorry. Of course. Tom.
S: Look, Barry, why don't you give me a call sometime? We could have lunch. You know – catch up.
B: Good idea! Let's do that.
S: Right … OK then … See you.
T: Bye now, Barry. Have a nice day!
B: Yes … urrh thanks. Speak to you soon, Susie.

Exercise 7

1 I really love the colour of your hair.
2 You're the most beautiful woman at the party!
3 You haven't phoned me for ages!
4 Congratulations on the birth of your baby!
5 Can I introduce you to my wife?
6 Did you hear the news this morning?
7 How are you getting on at the moment?
8 Please send my love to your family.
9 Your exam results are fantastic! Well done!
10 It's a lovely day, isn't it?

Lesson 9 Australia

Exercise 6

1 It'll be cheaper to buy a pass, if you plan several flights.
2 If you go in July and August, it won't be too hot.
3 You may even see dingoes – if you're very lucky.
4 Unless you like extremely hot weather, avoid December.

Lesson 10 Take it easy

Exercise 3

A = Astra   I = Ian

A: Ian! Come on! It's time to go to the gym! We'll be late.
I: I'm … uh … I'm not coming tonight.
A: Not coming?
I: No, I've decided to take the evening off. I think I've been taking on too much recently.
A: But I thought you enjoyed going?
I: Well, I did … I do, it's just …
A: But last week you said you were into getting fit.
I: Aah … yes … but now I can't stand it. In fact, I'm sick of running round the gym.
A: I don't understand.
I: Um, I think I've been taking it too seriously – I need a break.
A: This is ridiculous! You'll enjoy it when you get there.
I: Look, darling, I don't mind staying in and taking it easy for a change. You go without me. I'll be OK. Honestly.
[phone rings]

A: Hello … yes … yes … right … OK … I'll tell him. Bye.
I: Who was that?
A: It was Dave!
I: Dave?
A: Yeah … he says he's got a takeaway pizza and er … he'll be here in about 20 minutes …
I: Oh really?
A: … to watch the football match on TV with you!
I: But Astra, it is the big game.

Exercise 6

1 I was sick of being unfit so I took up aerobics.
2 We enjoy taking exercise, but we like taking it easy at other times.
3 It's quiet at six o'clock, so I don't mind getting up early to go running.
4 Are you keen on getting fit?
5 After I've done two hours' exercise, I need to take a break.
6 They love watching baseball on television.

Lesson 11 Determination

Exercise 4

S = Susan   T = Tim   B = Brenda   J = John

S: I used to live alone and I, urrh, got into the habit of eating chocolate, you know when I was watching TV and so on. I always used to enjoy it – a lot – but it was never a problem in the past. Then I found I was eating more and more – you know, I'd have some chocolate before meals, after meals and sometimes, even during meals. I put on more and more weight and I couldn't give it up. My friends noticed, too. One day, I decided to stop. It took a lot of willpower – but I must say, I feel better without the weight. I still miss chocolate though.

T: I used to love reading. I'd often read three books a week. Then they invented the Internet. I bought my first computer ten years ago and I immediately became completely addicted to it. Now I usually spend four hours a night on the Net. It's like having a best friend. I don't go out much and I don't have time to read any more – except the computer magazines, of course.

B: When I was at school I didn't use to do much sport. I'd often get my mother to give me a sick note so that I could miss the games lessons. It was only when I started work that I took an interest in exercise. I wanted to look good. There's a gym at work and I started going there. Now I go every day … I love it! In fact, it's about the only thing I do in my leisure time.

J: Smoking used to be quite acceptable … everyone did it when we were young, didn't they? Did you use to smoke? Anyway I smoked for years, 40 a day sometimes and I was totally dependent on it. But when I got married, my wife told me she hated the smell of cigarettes so I used hypnotherapy and quit smoking, for her.

Exercise 7

1 At school, I used to hate sport.
2 He used to go to Italy.
3 Did she use to go skiing a lot?

119

4 He didn't use to like computers.
5 Did she use to bite her nails?
6 I used to walk our dog every afternoon.

Lesson 13 The river

Exercise 4

A = Agent   T = Tourist

A: Good morning, Riverside Tours, Maria speaking. How can I help you?
T: Yes, hello. I have a reservation on the River Tour next week. I wonder if I could just check a few things?
A: Yes, of course. What's the reference number for your tour?
T: Um … oh yes, here it is, it's 334516.
A: 334516 … OK … the River Thames, two-day tour. How can I help you then?
T: Well, first, the departure time – what time does the boat actually set off from Kingston?
A: Nine o'clock, Monday morning. But we ask you to arrive about fifteen minutes before that.
T: Fine. So we set off at nine, and how long do we have at Hampton Court?
A: About four hours – the boat stops at Hampton Court around ten thirty and you spend about four hours there, including lunch. Then the tour carries on to Richmond and Kew Gardens in the afternoon.
T: Oh, that sounds great. What about that evening? First, what time do we arrive at the hotel?
A: At about five thirty.
T: And are there any plans for the evening?
A: Yes, there's a walking tour around the local area. It starts off at the hotel and carries on around the town. The walk starts at seven thirty but it's optional – so just tell the guide if you want to go or not.
T: Fine. I'm meeting a friend for dinner that night, so I think I'll miss that.
A: No problem. It's entirely optional.
T: What about the next day?
A: Well, on Tuesday, you set off again at ten o'clock and the tour takes you through the heart of London. You go past many famous sites: the Houses of Parliament, Tate Modern, Shakespeare's Globe Theatre … they're all listed in your brochure.
T: Yes, thank you. Just one more thing …
A: Yes, of course.
T: What time does the tour finish? I'm going to the theatre in the evening. I already have the tickets and I don't want to be late. It starts at eight o'clock.
A: You'll be fine. The tour finishes at Tower Bridge, at five thirty.
T: Well, that's all. Thanks for your help.
A: Not at all. Enjoy your trip.

Lesson 15 Less is more

Exercise 4

L = Laura   I = Interviewer

L: and there's never enough time!
I: I agree.
L: But you know … balance is the real answer.
I: Balance?
L: Well, take sleep … if you spend too much time asleep you're wasting an opportunity to use the time better, and it can actually make you more tired.

I: I never find my time in bed a wasted opportunity!
L: Well, I find a ten-minute nap in the afternoon gives me more energy than an extra hour in bed at night. You ought to try it.
I: OK. Laura, in your book, you, um, also say that we use too much technology.
L: That's right, we shouldn't forget that technology is for saving energy, not wasting it. We should all spend less time at the computer.
I: You seem to want less of everything!
L: In many ways, I do, yes. Take the work week, and I know this will sound strange, but I say we should work shorter hours …
I: That could be popular with many people.
L: Of course everyone wants to be successful, but people who work the longest hours have more stress, and so, achieve less.
I: Your position, then, is that less is more?
L: Exactly.
I: … and I suppose you're going to tell us that we eat too much, too?
L: Mmm … monkeys are healthier when they eat half their normal diet. If it works for them, perhaps we could try it too?
I: Although we're not monkeys, are we? Laura, sorry to stop you … I'd like to talk more but we appear to have less time than I thought. Laura Evans, thank you for spending time with us … And now for some more music …

Exercise 8

1 You could open the window for more fresh air.
2 Perhaps you ought to go to bed earlier.
3 You shouldn't watch horror movies before going to bed.
4 Perhaps you should do more exercise.
5 You should read a book in bed.
6 You shouldn't drink so much coffee.
7 Couldn't you try drinking warm milk?

Lesson 17 Changes

Exercise 5

I = Interviewer   G = Graham

I: Good morning and welcome to *Changing Cultures* our weekly look at ideas and beliefs from around the world. On last week's programme, Graham Ford, a computer analyst from London, agreed to try out some of the ideas behind Feng Shui. Welcome back Graham.
G: Thanks. It's nice to be here.
I: So Graham how did you get on? Has your life changed at all?
G: Well, I don't think Feng Shui has changed my life. Not yet anyway! But I've already tried one or two of the ideas from the article. For example I've just started running every morning and I feel a whole lot better!
I: Well fitness instructors have been telling us to do this for years!
G: Yeah, that's true!
I: What about some of the more unusual ideas? It says here that fish bring good luck. Have you bought any fish yet?
G: Well actually, I already owned a couple of goldfish, but they've never brought me much luck! Seriously though, I think some of the ideas in Feng Shui are really interesting. This thing about wearing grey, for example. I usually wear a lot of grey clothes, you know,

for work and so on, but I've just bought myself a new black suit and I feel much more decisive when I wear it.
I: Really? Yes, black does look very professional. So how about tidying your home and workplace every day … are you a tidy person Graham?
G: Not at all, no! Now that is something I'm going to try and do. I've already cleaned up my desk at work, it really helped me concentrate but I'm afraid I haven't started on the house yet. You see I've got two young kids, and my wife works too, so it's pretty hard to keep things tidy!
I: Thanks Graham. So listeners, what do you think? Has Feng Shui worked for you? Do you believe in it? Call us now on 0890-733-733 and tell us your views.

Lesson 18 How polite are you?

Exercise 7

1 A: Could you turn down your music?
   B: Yes, of course. Sorry.
2 A: Would you mind turning your music down, please?
   B: No, of course not.
3 A: Turn the music down a bit.
   B: OK.
4 A: Do you mind if I turn my music on?
   B: Not at all.

Lesson 19 Going alone

Exercise 8

1 I'd miss other people too much if I took part in the race.
2 He'd go out more if he knew more people.
3 I'd phone him if I knew his number.
4 If John were here, I'd ask him about the weekend.
5 If I wasn't scared of small spaces, I'd use the lift.
6 People would always understand me if I spoke English very well.

Lesson 20 What's in the fridge?

Exercise 4

T = Takanori   G = Gabriela

T: In my kitchen everything is extremely well-organised. My fridge is very modern and hi-tech. It's not quite big enough so I'm planning to get a larger one.
What do I keep in my fridge? Well, there's usually seafood, especially raw fish to make sushi – and I always have a good selection of fresh vegetables. Most of the food is Japanese, but I have some foreign things too … for example, I always keep a bottle of good French wine.
You can't afford to stand still in this business, you know always making the same dishes. That's why I've decided to visit some other countries, to get new ideas. But when I go, I won't waste time sightseeing, I'll try out new food. In fact, I hope to find some interesting, new Korean and Chinese recipes. My life is very busy you know and I work long hours so, when I have a free evening – and that's not very often – I spend time relaxing with friends or watching movies, never cooking!

G: My fridge is one of those large American ones, you know, with two doors. I've given up trying to keep it tidy and I keep on filling it so full that you can hardly shut the doors! So, what do I put in it? That's a good question. Well, there's always a selection of cold meat, cheese, ingredients for pasta, ice cream in the freezer, juices and other drinks … cans of beer for my teenage sons, the list goes on and on.

I avoid cooking complicated meals at home … I do enough of those at work. When friends visit, I don't make fantastic meals, no, I usually do something fast, like pasta. Sometimes they offer to do the cooking for me, which is great, because I really love other people's cooking!

Because I'm so busy, I don't often manage to have an evening off work. When I do, I sometimes go to restaurants, but never Italian ones! But I usually stay at home with my family and talk, and talk, and talk!

Lesson 21 Airport

Exercise 8

1 We really wanted a swim but we hadn't packed our swimsuits.
2 I decided to see the movie because I'd enjoyed the book so much.
3 As soon as I saw Rita, I realised I'd met her before.
4 After Marek had finished his homework, he went out with some friends.
5 When she asked to see my boarding card, I realised I'd lost it.
6 I knew I hadn't studied enough as soon as I saw the exam question.

Lesson 22 A star is born … or made?

Exercise 5

P = Presenter

P: My name's Phil Graham and welcome to *A Star is born … or made?* a look at stars, show business and fame. Take the Spice Girls for instance, one of the most successful bands of recent times, but how did it all start?

Imagine the scene, it's 1994. An advertisement is placed by a businessman in a British newspaper for five young women who can sing and dance. Thousands apply, hundreds are auditioned, and five are eventually chosen; Ginger, Posh, Scary, Sporty and … Michelle. Michelle?

Yes, Michelle soon decides that she'd rather go to college than be a Spice Girl, and leaves the group. Baby Spice, otherwise known as Emma Bunton, is asked to take her place.

It's now 1996, their first single, *Wannabe*, is released, and becomes a huge success. The hits keep on coming and the girls are soon known all over the world.

However, two years later, Geri Halliwell, or Ginger Spice, leaves the band because of disagreements with the others, and is later invited to be an ambassador by the United Nations.

Two of the 'girls', Posh Spice and Mel B, get married and have children. Surely this is the end of the most successful girl band in history? Not at all! Their fans love them even more. Posh Spice, and her famous footballer husband, David Beckham, together with their son Brooklyn, are regularly featured in newspapers and magazines all over the world.

So what do you think? Are they talented? Are they really stars? Or are they the creation of clever managers, talented songwriters and brilliant media manipulation? For me, they're pretty young women but without much talent. They are stars who are made by others. And despite their success, how long can the Spice Girls last? Where are they now as you listen to this?

Lesson 24 I'll call you

Exercise 3

R = Recording   D = Donna   G = Georgia

R: Good morning, Barnes Johnson … For Sales, press one. For Accounts, press two. For Enquiries, please hold.
D: Barnes Johnson. Thank you for calling. This is Donna speaking. How can I help you?
G: Hello, my name's Georgia King, I'd like to speak to Jon Barnes, please.
D: Sorry. What name is that?
G: It's Georgia King speaking.
D: Oh, I'm afraid Mr Barnes isn't here at the moment. Can I take a message?
G: Well, I'm returning his call. He left me a message to call him.
D: OK. Can you hold on, please … The line's busy at the moment. Can you call Mr Barnes back later?
G: Um … can I leave a message please?
D: Oh just a minute, I'll put you through to one of his colleagues. I'll just put you on hold …

Exercise 4

R = Recording   D = Donna   G = Georgia
C = Colleague   J = Jon

R: Good morning, Barnes Johnson … For Sales, press one. For Accounts, press two. For Enquiries, please hold.
D: Barnes Johnson. Thank you for calling. This is Donna speaking. How can I help you?
G: Hello, my name's Georgia King, I'd like to speak to Jon Barnes, please.
D: Sorry. What name is that?
G: It's Georgia King speaking.
D: Oh, I'm afraid Mr Barnes isn't here at the moment. Can I take a message?
G: Well, I'm returning his call. He left me a message to call him.
D: OK. Can you hold on, please … The line's busy at the moment. Can you call Mr Barnes back later?
G: Um … can I leave a message please?
D: Oh just a minute, I'll put you through to one of his colleagues. I'll just put you on hold …
C: Hello, Can I help you?
G: Hello. Yes, I'm trying to contact Jon Barnes.
C: Who's calling?
G: It's Georgia King … a friend of Jon's.
C: Is it a personal call?
G: Yes! I'm returning his call.
C: Ah. Just a moment.
J: Georgia! Is that you, Georgia …? Sorry to keep you waiting. I've been so busy. Look, I need to see you urgently!
C: Jon, there's a call for you on line two …
J: Oh no, Georgia, hang on a minute, don't hang up …

Exercise 8

1 I'd like to speak to Michael, please.
2 The line's busy.
3 I'm afraid she's not here at the moment.
4 Please hold on.
5 I'll just put you through.
6 Can I take a message?
7 I'm returning her call.
8 Could you call her back later?
9 It's me!

Lesson 26 Six and a half hours

Exercise 6

A You arrive at work tired. However, it could be a lot worse.
B Although he knows the journey time to the minute, he leaves nothing to chance.
C Despite many problems at work during the day, I've always forgotten them by the time I get home.
D Despite not enjoying the journey, he does not complain about it.
E In spite of staying with the same company all his life, he still only gets ten days off a year.

Lesson 27 Achievement

Exercise 3

A = Announcer   S = Susan Hunter

A: Later on this afternoon, in *Minds of our Time*, Susan Hunter will be discussing one of Britain's most famous inventors.
S: In many ways a typical inventor, Trevor Baylis is creative, outspoken, wild-haired and always working on new projects. Trevor is best known for his wind-up radio – which he developed in 1993 after realising that in many parts of Africa, people couldn't use radios because there was no electricity, and batteries were too expensive. He experimented at home and after only a few weeks came up with a working model. More recently, he's invented a wind-up torch and a wind-up computer.

Over the years, Trevor has won several prizes for his work but his search for inventions continues. Recently, he's been working on a power device which creates electricity as you walk. He hopes to use it to power a mobile phone. He has also been developing a wind-up system for roller-blades, but to find out more about this fascinating man, join us at four p.m.
A: And now we go over to …

Exercise 7

1 I haven't revised for my exam tomorrow, and now it's too late.
2 Mick's received a gold certificate for lifesaving.
3 I've been working on my typing skills, but I still make mistakes.
4 They're exhausted because they've been training for next week's marathon.
5 I've passed all my exams and now I'm going on holiday!
6 At last, I've finished working on that project.
7 He's been trying to get a new job but he hasn't had a single interview so far.

Lesson 28 Long walk to freedom

Exercise 2

N = Narrator

N: When I lay down, my head touched the wall at one end and my feet touched the wall at the other end. The room was about six feet wide. I was 46 years old, a political prisoner with a life sentence, and that small space was going to be my home for a long time. The first week we began the work. Each morning, we were given hammers and had to break stones. Warders walked among us and made us work in silence. The work was boring, and difficult. At noon we would break for lunch. That first week all we were given was soup. In the afternoon, we were allowed to exercise for half an hour, under strict supervision.

Exercise 8

1 Mandela's prison warders only let him exercise for 30 minutes a day.
2 In the past, many prisoners were made to wear chains.
3 Our family was very relaxed about rules, and I was allowed to come home any time I wanted.
4 My grandmother was very strict – she didn't let us talk at the dinner table at her house.
5 My parents gave me no choice. I had to keep my room tidy.
6 There was a 'no smoking' rule at my school. The teachers and the students weren't allowed to smoke anywhere.
7 Some warders were kind. They didn't make me work when I was ill.

Lesson 29 Shaking hands

Exercise 4

I = Interviewer N = Nancy Fairweather

I: Good evening and welcome to this week's edition of *Business Today*. These days we're all doing business in a global market, dealing with partners in many different countries. We need to be careful not to say or do the wrong thing, offend someone and risk losing an important deal. To help us look at this issue, we have Nancy Fairweather, a cultural adviser, with us in the studio. So, Nancy, what advice can you give us?
N: Well, you probably won't have so many problems if you travel close to home. But a bit further away, for example in the Middle East, you need to be more careful. I haven't been there myself, but if I visited an office there, they would almost certainly offer me a hot drink, either coffee or mint tea. Don't expect to do things in a hurry, though. If I wanted to negotiate a deal there, I would expect it to take some time.
I: You mentioned coffee and mint tea. What about food and drink? It's a difficult area, isn't it?
N: It can be, yes. We all know, for example, that in the UK if someone invites you to the pub, they'll expect you to buy some drinks, which seems strange for many cultures!
I: Yes, indeed.
N: And business lunches are very different around the world too. In the US, if you have a business lunch, it'll probably only last an hour. And there are bigger surprises for you in the US.
I: Oh really? Tell us more.
N: Well, you should always be punctual for meetings, and this seems very formal, but then they'll usually call everyone by their first name.
I: Right! I'll remember that one. What about present-giving? That can be a problem, can't it?
N: Yes. There's the issue of whether to give a present or not. In the US, if you gave them a present, they'd probably think it was a bribe. Then, if you do receive a present, should you open it immediately or not? If you gave a present in Thailand, they wouldn't open it straightaway. It's also very important to know what to give.
I: And what not to give of course. Tell us more about …

Lesson 30 Sunshine and showers

Exercise 5

G = Grandmother F = Friend
W = Weatherman

G: There's an old saying, 'Red sky at night, shepherd's delight. Red sky in the morning, shepherd's warning.' Now, the sky was very red this morning, so it's a warning that there will be rain. I feel sure about this because the cows are lying down in the fields too, and that's another sure sign of wet weather. So it'll rain for most of the day … I'm sorry about that. You'll just have to have the party inside. I'm sure it'll be nice.

F: Well, I think we have to try and listen to our feelings. If you want to try and predict the weather, well, you need to listen to your body and your dreams. Dreams can really tell us a lot. I've been dreaming about the colour blue a lot recently. That's usually a good sign. And last night I was lying on a tropical beach. It felt very warm, and there were blue skies. And that can mean only one thing – lots of warm weather and sunshine. Trust me, I'm never wrong.

W: Good evening. The weather for tomorrow is looking very changeable. There's cold weather coming down from Canada and there'll be rain and strong winds in the next 24 hours. And if we look at the satellite images from this morning, the grey circles here show that thunderstorms are on the way. They will probably be everywhere by the morning and temperatures will be below average. That's all for now. We'll be back with another weather report after the late news.

Exercise 6

G = Grandmother F = Friend S = Steve

G: I told them the sky had been very red that morning and that it would rain. I also told them that the cows were lying down in the fields and that was another sign of rain. I predicted it would rain for most of the day. So I was about right, wasn't I?

F: I told them you need to listen to your dreams. I said I'd been dreaming about blue and that the night before I'd dreamed about a beach. I said my dream could only mean one thing: sunshine. Well, I guess I was wrong … but nobody's perfect.

S: The weatherman was right when he said it was looking changeable. He said that there'd be rain and winds in the following 24 hours, and that thunderstorms were on the way. He also predicted that cold weather was coming down from the north. I think we should have listened to the weather report after all.

Lesson 33 Tomorrow's world

Exercise 4

1 Methods of communication are advancing rapidly – by 2035, scientists will have perfected the 'brainlink' computer. A tiny computer will be implanted under your skin on the back of your head. It will tell your brain how to speak any language you need.
2 The number of robots is increasing all the time. By 2020, there could be more robots than people in developed countries. Computers could be connected to our brains by 2025. The number of schools will fall or they may even disappear completely. You will simply be able to download information into your head.
3 By 2020, scientists will have produced computers that you can eat – one per day. They will record everything that's going on inside you and carry this information to a small box that you wear on your belt. These systems will be invaluable to doctors.
4 The boundaries between people and machines will eventually disappear. By 2050, scientists will have developed a technique for implanting chips in our brains. These will allow us to communicate by simply using our brainwaves.

Lesson 34 Honeymoon horrors

Exercise 4

R = Radio announcer M = Mike C = Caz
N = Neil W = Wendy

R: When most people think about honeymoons, they think of exotic holidays in beautiful places – the perfect start to a new life together. However, we spoke to four people whose holidays of a lifetime turned into honeymoon horrors …
M: Well, we went on safari to Tanzania for our honeymoon. It was fantastic until one day when we were out looking for elephants I stood on a snake. I didn't see it until it was too late, and it bit me on the leg … it started to swell up straightaway. I thought I was going to pass out. Luckily my wife got me to a hospital where I got treatment. After that, I was OK but my leg ached for three months. I'd never go back.
C: I was at the beach off the north coast of Australia, when suddenly a jellyfish swam near me and touched my leg. It stung me all down the side of my left leg. I screamed and my husband ran in and pulled me out of the water. My whole leg had come out in huge red spots. Lucky there was a hospital nearby or it might have turned into something worse.
N: We were on honeymoon in Ecuador and I had forgotten to take my malaria tablets. One day I was bitten by a mosquito on my neck.

It was very itchy but I didn't pay much attention to it really. Two days later my whole body ached. I didn't know what I'd come down with. After I had some injections at the hospital, I started to feel better but I was still really tired.

W: My husband and I went camping in the USA after we got married. One evening, a spider crawled into our tent and bit my arm. I was in agony – it really, really hurt. I had a very high fever and threw up several times. It took me almost a year to get over it, and to get completely better but I'll never go camping again!

R: So how can you prevent the holiday of a lifetime turning into a nightmare?

Exercise 7

1 I thought I was going to pass out.
2 It started to swell up straightaway.
3 My whole leg had come out in huge red spots.
4 It might have turned into something worse.
5 I didn't know what I'd come down with.
6 I threw up several times.
7 It took me almost a year to get over it.

Lesson 37 Old friends

Exercise 4

J = James   R = Richard

J: Richard is my oldest friend. I've known him for 60 years. We first met when Richard started at my school. We've kept in touch since then and we've never lost contact with each other. We've remained good friends throughout our lives. Richard was my best man when I got married and he's helped me a lot since I lost my wife, Dora …
We both lived in London in the 1970s but we didn't see much of each other – I suppose we were busy with our jobs and families. We've both been living in Brighton since we retired in 1995, so it's good to get together to remember the old days. I suppose I see him about once a month, either for a drink in the evening or sometimes in the park. Yes, we've been going to the park for a long time now.

R: I've known James for about 55 years. We first met when he moved to my town. He went to a different school but we became friends because he lived next door to me. We've known each other since then, but we haven't kept in touch all that time … we lost contact with each other when I moved to Scotland in the 1970s for my job … I didn't go to James' wedding, but he came to mine … .. And now? Well, I've been living here in Brighton since '99, and these days I see James about once a week, usually in the park where I walk my dog, or in the pub for lunch with another friend that we've known for about the same length of time. We haven't been doing that for very long but it's good to get all of us together.

Exercise 8

1 We've known them for more than twenty years.
2 She's won the competition for the last five years.
3 Have you visited your grandmother since her accident?

4 They haven't phoned me for ages.
5 I've been doing my homework for two hours.
6 I've liked her for a long time.
7 How long have you been living here?

Lesson 38 Don't worry, be happy

Exercise 4

W = Woman   M = Man

W: Ah, good morning. Excuse me, Sir…
M: Yes …?
W: We're doing a survey.
M: Sorry, I can't stop, I'm in a hurry.
W: Just a minute of your time …
M: But … I really haven't got time.
W: It won't take long. We're doing a 'happiness' survey; to find out how happy people think they are.
M: Well, if it's very, very quick.
W: Thank you. First, would you mind telling me if you've ever seen the doctor about being depressed?
M: Oh, that's a very personal question, isn't it? Umm, I think I'd rather not say.
W: Yes, of course. Right … well, could you tell me which you worry about more – health or money?
M: Oh no, I'd prefer not to answer that one either. Look, if these are the kinds of questions, um, I think I'll …
W: No, no, no, the others are different. What about number three? Can I ask if you are married?
M: Yes, I am.
W: And, er, can I ask you how you feel about your marriage?
M: Well, I'm very pleased with my marriage, actually!
W: That's nice, and next um, I'd like to know how you feel about your job.
M: Well, I'm glad to have a job, but I do worry about it sometimes.
W: Aha. And can I ask you what exactly you worry about?
M: Well, I worry most, about being late. Oh no, look at the time! Now I am late thanks to you! Goodbye.
W: Sorry. Thank you for your – er – time.

Exercise 9

1 I'd like to know if you're generally an optimistic person.
2 Can I ask if you are happy with your job?
3 Could you tell me if you woke up in a good mood this morning?
4 I'd like to know how you'd react if someone damaged your car.
5 Would you mind telling me how you'd feel about winning the lottery?
6 Could you tell me if you worry about getting old?
7 Can I ask you if you like answering personal questions?

Lesson 40 How did it go?

Exercise 3

I = Interviewer   M = Madeline   H = Harry

I: Thank you very much indeed for coming, Miss Sharp. A very interesting interview. I'd be grateful if you could just wait a few minutes. Do take a seat here in reception.

M: Yes, of course. Thank you very much.
H: So, how did it go?
M Oh, I don't know. I think I made a mess of it.
H: Oh, I'm sure you didn't …
M: She asked me so many questions.
H: What did she ask you?
M: Well, she asked me what experience I had. In fact, she asked me about all my previous jobs … and why I'd left them … and what kind of responsibilities I'd had. I kept talking about things which weren't really relevant to the job. I couldn't remember which bit of my experience I needed to talk about …
H: I'm sure you were fine.
M: Oh, I don't know. I think I talked a lot of rubbish really.
H: What else did she ask you?
M: Well, she wanted to know what my strengths and weaknesses were.
H: That's a tough question – your weaknesses, I mean.
M: Yes, I couldn't think how to answer it at first, but then, I thought it was best to say something that a lot of people have.
H: Good idea.
M: Yes, I said I was too much of a perfectionist.
H: Oh, that was a good one. Well done.
M: Yes, but I got nervous because she wanted to know what my other weaknesses were too. I think I said too much. I said that sometimes I forget things. Maybe I shouldn't have said that – I was just trying to be honest. Oh …
H: What else?
M: She wanted me to tell her if I could work under pressure, and I said I could, but I don't think she believed me.
H: Oh, I'm sure you were fine. Did you ask any questions?
M: Umm … I think I made a mess of that too! I asked how many breaks you get in a day.
H: Oh, I don't think that was a very good question, sounds like you prefer breaks to work.
M: Oh dear. I think you're right.
I: Miss Sharp, I'm very sorry to keep you waiting. I just had to check one or two things. I'm delighted to say we'd like to offer you the job.
M: Oh, thank you, that's marvellous!
I: If you've got a few minutes now, perhaps we can discuss …

1 It's absolutely true!

1 1 awful 2 exhausted 3 crowded 4 big
5 enormous 6 packed 7 tired
8 fantastic

2 1 stopped; were driving
2 was laughing; dropped
3 arrived; was serving
4 took; was getting
5 was dancing; broke

3 1 were walking
2 decided
3 told
4 was stealing
5 was looking
6 arrested
7 took
8 were examining
9 was laughing

2 Are you a morning person?

1 1 Leila wants a lie <u>in</u>.
2 Walter <u>wakes up</u> early.
3 Ellie is an early <u>riser</u>.
4 Sam sometimes <u>oversleeps</u> and is late for work.
5 Mandy had an early <u>night</u> last night.
6 Ronald got out of <u>bed</u> on the wrong side.
7 Kurt can't keep his eyes <u>open</u>.
8 Stella likes to <u>stay</u> up late to watch films.

2 1 What language do Italians speak?
2 Who built the Colosseum?
3 Where does pasta come from?
4 Who lives in the Vatican City?
5 Where does Roma football team play?
6 What do Italians drink for breakfast?

3 1 c 2 g 3 d 4 f 5 e 6 a

3 What's in a name?

1 1 d 2 f 3 h 4 e 5 g 6 c 7 a

2 1 <u>She's going to go</u> to Spain.
2 I don't think <u>I'll buy it</u> now, thanks.
3 <u>We're going to call</u> her Petra.
4 Aren't you <u>going to take</u> that new job?
5 <u>Will he go</u> with us, or not?
6 <u>I don't think</u> they're going to go.
7 OK, then. Tell Amy <u>I'll meet her</u> later.

3 1 Are you going to see; I am
2 are you going to give; I'll think
3 I'm going to have; I'll have
4 We're going to get; Are you going to have
5 I'm going to go shopping; I'll come
6 Are you going to go; I'm not

4 Career paths

1 1 left (h) 2 go (f) 3 took (b) 4 passed (c)
5 grades (i) 6 university (a) 7 exams (e)
8 degree (g)

2 1 Ben was more successful than Anna.
2 Anna got the worst grades.
3 Carly got higher grades than Ben.
4 Carly got the best grades.
5 Anna was the least successful.

3 1 Maria <u>is the fastest</u> swimmer in the team.
2 Your house is a lot <u>bigger</u> than mine.
3 The weather <u>is much worse</u> than it was yesterday.

4 Gina is the <u>most successful</u> person in our class.
5 She's the <u>best</u> teacher in the whole school.
6 My brother is <u>the tallest</u> person in our family.

5 On the other hand

1 1 no trouble 2 straightforward 3 tough
4 no trouble 5 simple

2 1 can use 2 Can you 3 are able to
4 can't use 5 can't read 6 managed to

3 1 I can't eat spicy food.
2 My dad is able to speak five languages.
3 We haven't managed to see the baby yet.
4 I forgot my camera so I wasn't able to take any photos.
5 It was expensive but I was able to pay with my credit card.
6 It was difficult but I managed to finish it.

6 Corporate spying

1

2 1 I study hard in order to learn English fast.
2 She drives carefully so as not to have an accident.
3 Marco carries a dictionary for checking vocabulary when he's reading.
4 Take an umbrella in case it rains.
5 She always carries her phone so that she can call her friends.
6 Write it down in case you forget it.
7 I watch the news in English to get listening practice.

3 1 In winter, I wear a hat in order to keep warm.
2 He leaves his house at 6.30 so as not to be late for work.
3 Take my phone number in case you want to phone me.
4 She needs a computer for working at home.

7 Teamwork

1 *getting a different job:*
apply for a job
get a promotion
go for an interview
using an office machine:
send an e-mail
use a computer
receive a fax
other work activities:
organise an event
write a report
work in a team

2 1 Have you done
2 I have
3 I've worked

4 I was
5 were you
6 I wasn't
7 has had
8 you haven't
9 I haven't
10 you've had

3 1 Have you ever <u>eaten</u> Indian food?
2 He's never worked in an office, <u>has he</u>?
3 Correct
4 Have you ever <u>lied</u> to your boss?
5 We <u>bought</u> a new computer yesterday.
6 Correct
7 They <u>flew</u> on Concorde in 1999.
8 Correct

8 Nice to meet you

1 1 Bye bye 2 This is Ron 3 Hello
4 the weather 5 well done 6 criticising

2 a) Frances, this is Charlie.
b) Let me introduce you to everyone.
c) See you at 1.30 then.
d) How are you and your family?
e) Good to see you here again.
f) How was the journey?
g) I love your dress!
h) But the food was terrible.

3 1 e 2 d 3 f 4 h 5 b 6 a 7 g 8 c

9 Australia

1 a) rain clothes
b) sleeping bag
c) sun cream
d) money belt
e) mosquito repellent
f) first-aid kit
g) walking boots
h) water bottle
i) guide book

2 1 f 2 h 3 a 4 g 5 d 6 e 7 b 8 c

3 1 will be; come
2 go; will be
3 phone; 'll tell
4 will you do; doesn't come
5 help; won't finish
6 does; 'll ask

10 Take it easy

1 1 break 2 on 3 off 4 easy 5 up

2 1 Why don't you <u>take the day off</u>?
2 The exam finishes at 2.30, then you can <u>take a break</u> for an hour.
3 You can <u>take part</u> in many outdoor activities on this holiday.
4 Last year, I <u>took on</u> too much and I got very tired.
5 I've got more time now, so I'm going to <u>take up</u> a new hobby.

3 1 My brother's really <u>into</u> rollerskating.
2 Are you keen <u>on</u> going to the cinema?
3 I don't mind <u>doing</u> my homework.
4 He's sick <u>of</u> doing the dishes.
5 Mandy <u>can't</u> stand playing the violin.
6 I don't want <u>to</u> go to work today.
7 She <u>doesn't</u> mind walking to work.
8 He isn't keen on <u>watching</u> football.
9 She enjoys <u>playing</u> tennis.

11 Determination

1 1 addictive
2 determination
3 cutting down
4 to give up
5 shopping
6 dependent

2 1 did you use to
2 used to
3 did you use to
4 didn't use to
5 Did you use to
6 used to

3 1 He used to live with his parents but now he's married.
2 He didn't use to have any children but now he has a daughter.
3 He used to have a skateboard but now he has a car.
4 He used to play the guitar, but now he plays golf.
5 He didn't use to wear glasses but now he does.

12 Money matters

1 1 g 2 i 3 a 4 e 5 h
6 j 7 k 8 d 9 f 10 b

2 1 They told us the news.
2 He brought me a present from Indonesia.
3 Could you please show it to me?
OR Could you show it to me, please?
4 My teacher taught us some vocabulary.
5 You can always ask me for help.
6 Please order me a chicken curry.
OR Order me a chicken curry, please.
7 I was lost so she drew me a map.
8 Don't forget to send me a postcard.

13 The river

1 1 ... it went on for four hours.
2 My car broke down twice last week.
3 Could you put me up tonight?
4 We set off early so the traffic wasn't very busy.
5 ... I carried on by bus.

2 1 f 2 h 3 c 4 e 5 g 6 a 7 d 8 b

3 1 Are you doing
2 'm meeting
3 'm staying
4 finish
5 'm going
6 Are you doing
7 'm going
8 leaves
9 'm going
10 'm getting up

14 Radio wedding

1 1 groom 2 reception 3 fiancé
4 civil 5 fiancée 6 best man
7 religious 8 ceremony 9 honeymoon

2 1 over 2 back 3 with 4 know

3 1 ... they got engaged.
2 I get on well with ....
3 She got upset when ....
4 ... now we've got back together.
5 ... an opportunity to get to know each other.

15 Less is more

1 1 b 2 d 3 e 4 g 5 a 6 c

2 1 You <u>shouldn't</u> worry about ...
2 Perhaps you could <u>try</u> walking ...
3 I think you ought to <u>take</u> ...
4 Perhaps you <u>ought not to</u> use ...
5 Perhaps <u>you could</u> plan ...
6 You <u>shouldn't</u> eat ...

3 1 You should go to the doctor.
2 You ought not to go to work.
3 Perhaps you could stay in bed.
4 You shouldn't get cold.

16 Looks good!

1 Across: 2 touch 5 taste 7 sound
Down: 1 sight 3 hearing 4 feel 6 look

2 1 who / that 2 when / no relative pronoun
3 who / that 4 whose
5 that / no relative pronoun 6 which / that

3 1 What's the name of that couple who have six children?
2 Put it in the office where Robert works.
3 Where's that parcel which / that was delivered this morning?
4 There's a film on tonight which / that / no relative pronoun you might like.
5 This is the plane which / that carries over 450 people.

17 Changes

1 1 noise – noisy
2 wealth – wealthy
3 good health – healthy
4 success – successful
5 stress – stressful

2 a) I've just done it.
b) No, she hasn't moved yet.
c) No thanks. I've already eaten.
d) I don't know. I haven't read it yet.
e) No, I haven't seen it recently.
f) Yes, they've decided to make the changes.

3 1 a 2 d 3 c 4 f 5 e 6 b

18 How polite are you?

1 1 ... could you <u>turn it up</u>?
2 correct
3 If you turn <u>on</u> the radio ...
4 ... if you switch them <u>on</u>.
5 correct
6 ... be sure to turn all the lights <u>off</u>.
7 We switch the heating <u>on</u> at ...
8 ... then turn it <u>off</u>.

2 1 Would you mind coming early tomorrow?
2 Can you speak up a bit?
3 Could you say that again?
4 Do you mind if I go now?
5 Could you tell me the time?
6 Can you phone me with the results, please?
7 Would you mind helping me with my homework?

3 1 Could you move your car, please?
2 Do you mind not interrupting me again?
3 Can you give me a lift into town?
4 Do you mind not smoking in here?
5 Please could you make less noise?
6 Would you mind waiting for me?

19 Going alone

1a

1b 1 lonely 2 alone 3 worried 4 nervous

2 1 got
2 didn't open
3 wouldn't panic
4 'd try
5 had
6 'd phone
7 would you do
8 wouldn't be
9 was
10 'd scream

3 1 If he had time, he'd finish the report today.
2 I'd buy a horse if I didn't live in a city.
3 If I studied harder, I wouldn't always fail my exams.
4 I'd be very rich if I knew the winning lottery numbers.
5 If I had a yacht, I could go sailing at weekends.
6 I'd do things differently if I could live my life over again.

20 What's in the fridge?

1 1 My father is a <u>cook</u> in a restaurant.
2 It'll be a <u>three-course</u> dinner: soup, meat and dessert.
3 What time do you have your biggest <u>meal</u> of the day?
4 My sister is a vegan, so she <u>doesn't</u> eat eggs.
5 You should always keep ice cream in the <u>freezer</u>.
6 I used to be a <u>vegetarian</u>, but now I eat meat and fish.
7 Put the carrots in water and <u>boil</u> them for ten minutes.

2 1 eating 2 to buy 3 smoking 4 to pass
5 playing 6 to have 7 to clear up
8 interrupting

3 1 talking 2 to go 3 smoking 4 saying
5 going 6 watching 7 to meet 8 to be
9 to make

21 Airport

1 1 e (cabin crew)
2 g (departure lounge)
3 d (check-in desk)
4 a (boarding card)
5 c (duty free shops)
6 h (flight information screens)
7 b (passport control)
8 f (hand luggage)

2 1 arrived; had already started
2 wanted; hadn't opened
3 'd forgotten; pushed
4 wanted; 'd seen
5 realised; 'd organised

3 A: 1 d 2 b 3 c 4 a
B: 1 d 2 a 3 b 4 c

22 A star is born ... or made?

1 1 skilful 2 brilliant 3 fashionable
4 original 5 successful 6 talented

2 1 left 2 found 3 had frozen
4 was invented 5 was sold 6 are known
7 was made 8 be removed 9 be carried
10 have bought 11 is seen

23 The future of toys

1 1 c (board game)
2 f (computer game)
3 e (dolls)
4 b (jigsaw puzzle)
5 d (cards)
6 a (skateboard)

2 1 I <u>might</u> not take the exam this year.
2 I'm sure you <u>will</u> like the new job.
3 I doubt if <u>he'll arrive</u> late.
4 He <u>doesn't</u> think it'll rain tomorrow.
5 We <u>won't go</u> without you.
6 I <u>expect</u> I'll go by train.

3 1 John might be late today.
2 I'll be a scientist or a doctor.
3 He might go skiing this year.
4 My boss won't cancel the meeting.
5 Anne may be able to help you.
6 I might go on studying English.
7 He may phone the doctor today.
8 The job could start on Monday.

24 I'll call you

1 2 hang 3 this 4 answer 5 texting
6 return 7 press 8 pay phone 9 mobile
10 on 11 make
Mystery word: answerphone

2 1A: Hi, it's Ana. Can I speak to Rita.
   B: I'm afraid she's not here at the moment.
2A: Can I leave a message, please?
   B: Yes, of course.
3A: Hello, I'd like to speak to the manager, please.
   B: Hold on, I'll see if he's here. Who's speaking?
4A: It's Jun Fuji. I'm returning his call.
   B: I'll try and put you through now.
5A: I'm afraid the line's busy at the moment.
   B: In that case, I'll call him back later.

25 Do the right thing

1 1 do 2 make 3 Do 4 make 5 do
6 make

2 1 f 2 d 3 e 4 a 5 c 6 b

3 1 I don't have to get up early on Saturday.
2 You should try to remember friends' birthdays.
3 We mustn't copy other students' answers in exams.
4 You don't have to pay for library books.
5 ... I have to do more homework.
6 You mustn't drink and drive.

26 Six and a half hours

1 1 ... are carefully <u>timed</u>.
2 I had <u>a</u> really good time at the office party.
3 I think sitting in a traffic jam is a waste <u>of</u> time.
4 I love having <u>time off</u>, when I don't have to go to work.
5 By <u>the time</u> I get home ...
6 I always arrive for work <u>on time</u>.

2 1 despite / in spite of 2 Although
3 Despite not 4 Although 5 However
6 Despite / In spite of 7 despite / in spite of

3 1 The morning break is fifteen minutes.
   However, you take twenty.
2 Although lunch finishes at 12.30, you never come back on time.
3 In spite of this being a non-smoking office, you smoke all the time.
4 There are three weeks paid holiday.
   However, you take extra time off.
5 Although employees cannot make personal phone calls, you make a lot.
6 Despite work not finishing until 5.30, you always leave early.

27 Achievement

1 Across: 6 certificate 7 prize 8 examination
Down: 1 project 2 ambition 3 skill
       4 doctor 5 device

2 1 to achieve an ambition
2 to receive a certificate
3 to win a prize
4 to revise for an examination
5 to train to be a doctor
6 to develop a skill
7 to invent a device
8 to solve a problem

3 1 've been playing
2 Have you reached
3 's been cooking
4 's made
5 've been trying
6 've been going
7 Have you been running

28 Long walk to freedom

1 1 They didn't let anybody gamble in the bar.
   – Sign D
2 People had to take off their dirty boots.
   – Sign B
3 They made men leave their guns outside.
   – Sign F
4 They didn't let any children in the place.
   – Sign C
5 Horses had to be kept outside. – Sign E

2 1 did you have to pay
2 didn't make me pay
3 had to pay
4 wasn't allowed to bring
5 made me leave
6 let me phone

29 Shaking hands

1 1 b; c 2 a; c 3 b; c
4 a; b 5 b; c 6 a; c

2 1 d 2 g 3 e 4 a 5 c 6 f 7 b

3 1 If I get a pay rise next week, I'll buy a new TV.
2 If he failed his exam, he would take it again.
3 I'd go to the party if I didn't feel sick.
4 If it rains tomorrow, I won't walk to work.
5 He'd send her an e-mail if he knew her e-mail address.

30 Sunshine and showers

1 1 heavy rain 2 light showers 3 thick fog
4 bright sunshine 5 strong wind
6 heavy snow 7 severe thunderstorm

2 1 'I'll invite you to my party'.
2 'I don't care what you've done.'

3 'I stayed with Sandra last night.'
4 'We can't come to the meeting tomorrow.'

3 1 They said they were very happy with the hotel room.
2 She told me she would be glad when it was all finished.
3 He told us we could start the race when he said "Go".
4 They said they were going to leave the next day / the day after / the following day.

31 Turning points

1 1 b (magazine)
2 e (novel)
3 g (poetry)
4 a (best-seller)
5 h (text book)
6 f (website)
7 c (newspapers)

2 1 b 2 d 3 f 4 j 5 a 6 k 7 c 8 g 9 i 10 e

3 1 left; had been living
2 missed; had been looking
3 had been hoping; rained
4 had been standing; found
5 had been expecting; arrived

32 Clean and tidy

1 1 housework; tidy
2 messy
3 washing; dishes
4 vacuum; dust

2 1 ... but today I cut <u>myself</u>.
2 She <u>washed</u> and went out ...
3 ... they really enjoyed <u>themselves</u>.
4 ... lights turn <u>themselves</u> off at midnight.
5 correct
6 Do you ever talk to <u>yourself</u>?

3 1 Did you have it delivered?
2 No, actually. I cooked it myself.
3 Did you make them too?
4 No, I had them made.
5 Do you develop the photos yourself?
6 Shall I have one sent to your room?
7 No, I can get it myself.
8 You can do it yourself, or I can have it done for you.

33 Tomorrow's world

1

2 2 d By June 14th we will have lived here for ten years.
3 e ... and then I will have read all her books.
4 a We will have flown for fourteen hours non-stop by the time this flight lands.
5 c ... so they will have been married for 50 years
6 b ... his train will have reached Rome.

3 1 ... I will have <u>worked</u> here for three years.
2 correct
3 ... we will <u>have known</u> each other for six months.
4 ... exam <u>by</u> next July?
5 ..., I will <u>have gone</u> to the airport.
6 correct

34 Honeymoon horrors

1 1 itchy 2 bitten 3 stung 4 swollen
5 stings 6 swelling 7 aches 8 biting

2 1 He saw the blood and passed <u>out</u> immediately.
2 He's gone to bed – he doesn't want his headache to turn <u>into</u> something worse.
3 correct
4 Oh, what a mess! He's thrown <u>up</u> all over the carpet!
5 correct
6 When he eats peanuts, his tongue swells <u>up</u>.
7 correct
8 He feels terrible. He thinks he's coming <u>down</u> with something.
9 A fever sometimes makes you come <u>out in</u> a sweat.

35 Ice maiden

1 1 status 2 generation 3 culture 4 people
5 team 6 family

2 1 could they have been
2 might have made
3 might have represented
4 could have used
5 might have shown
6 must have made

3 1 I must have lost it.
2 They can't have heard it.
3 They might / could have been on holiday.
4 She can't have studied enough.
5 He might / could have forgotten.

36 A winning formula

1
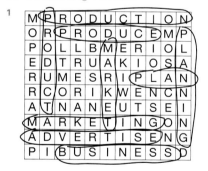

2 1 market 2 product 3 plan 4 produce
5 marketing 6 advertise 7 production
8 business plan 9 business 10 planning
11 product

3 1 The new marketing director, whose wife works in finance, is arriving tomorrow.
2 In my teenage years, when I thought life was easy, I used to play sport all day.
3 New Orleans, where jazz is very popular, is in southern USA.
4 My mother, who is 75 now, had a lovely birthday party.
5 The bank manager, whose name I can never remember, wants to see me on Monday.
6 My mobile, which I always have with me, keeps me in touch with the office.

37 Old friends

1 1 made 2 are in touch 3 lost 4 keep
5 send 6 keep up 7 rely on 8 remain

2

for	since
a) b) e) g) l)	c) d) f) h) i) j) k) m) n)

3 1 I've been travelling in Australia since last week / for a week.
2 He hasn't ridden a bicycle since he was thirteen / for twelve years.
3 Have you been here since the beginning of the movie?
4 Raul's been feeling ill for three hours.
5 She hasn't contacted me for ages.
6 They've known each other for six months.

38 Don't worry, be happy

1

2 1 Would you mind telling me when your birthday is?
2 Can I ask you what your weight is?
3 Could you tell me how much you earn?
4 I would like to know if you are happy.
5 Could you tell me how much coffee you drink?
6 Would you mind telling me if you eat meat?

3 1 I'd like to know if you are happy in your work.
2 Could you tell me what keeps you awake at night?
3 Would you mind telling me what you do in the evenings?
4 Can I ask you how much you spend on cigarettes?
5 Would you mind telling me what makes you depressed?
6 I'd like to know if you are free at the weekend.
7 Would you mind telling me where you usually go for your holidays?

39 If only ...

1 1 try clothes on
2 browse
3 buy things on impulse
4 the sales
5 take things back
6 haggle
7 refund
8 go window shopping
9 get a bargain

2 1 would never have met
2 hadn't slipped
3 wouldn't have broken
4 hadn't broken
5 wouldn't have met
6 had been
7 wouldn't have looked after
8 hadn't met
9 wouldn't have fallen
10 wouldn't have got

3 1 If (only) I'd taken your advice, I wouldn't have paid too much.
2 If (only) I'd taken a map, I wouldn't have got lost.
3 If (only) she hadn't switched her phone off, she would have got my message.
4 If (only) I'd travelled first class, I wouldn't have had a terrible flight.
5 If (only) I hadn't been rude to my boss, I wouldn't have lost my job.

40 How did it go?

1 1 qualifications 2 long-term goals
3 promotion 4 prospects 5 references
6 experience 7 strengths 8 weaknesses
9 interview

2 1 ... what software <u>I had used</u>.
2 ... to know if <u>I could drive</u>.
3 ... the woman asked me if <u>I had any questions</u>.
4 I asked them <u>if I was allowed</u> to smoke.
5 They asked <u>me if I could start next</u> month.
6 ... one of the men wanted to know when I <u>could give them</u> my decision.

127

Pearson Education Limited
Edinburgh Gate, Harlow
Essex CM20 2JE, England
and Associated Companies throughout the world.

www.language-to-go.com

Language to go is a trademark of Pearson Education Limited

© Pearson Education Limited 2002

First published 2002
Fourth impression 2004
Set in 9/12pt Neue Helvetica Medium and 9/12pt Univers Light
Printed in Spain by Mateu Cromo, S.A. Pinto (Madrid)
ISBN 0 582 40398 7

Author acknowledgements

The authors would like to say a huge thank you to the ace team at Longman for all their hard work and understanding throughout the project, especially Judith King, Caroline Mapus-Smith and Frances Woodward. Thanks also to Steve Pitcher, Eddi Edwards, Catriona Watson-Brown, Yolanda Durham and Rose Wells and all the others who have contributed to the book. We would also like to thank Simon Greenall for his perception and overall vision. And special thanks to Bernie Hayden for his tireless energy, thoughtful comments and good humour. There are a number of people who gave their time and real-life inspiration to some of the tapescripts in the book – thanks to Mychael Barratt, Jeremy Page, Sara Perry, and Joe Wileman.

On a more personal note, a big thank you to Minty's mother, Gay, and Robin's children, Matilda, Georgia, Joe and Tim for all their continued support, encouragement and practical help. We would also like to thank Richard Acklam for giving us invaluable advice at all stages of the project, and Martin Parrott for his ever-positive attitude. And not least, thanks to our lovely daughters, Petra (age 5) and Lola (age 3), for putting up with us while writing was in progress!

Publishing acknowledgements

The publishers would like to extend thanks to the freelance editorial team. We are indebted to Bernie Hayden, Senior Development Editor for the whole series, for his outstanding contribution to *Language to go*. Special thanks are due to Catriona Watson-Brown for her editorial guidance and assistance, including her work on the Phrasebooks which accompany each level of the series. We would also like to acknowledge with thanks Kenna Bourke for her writing of the Grammar reference.

The publishers and authors are very grateful to the following people and institutions for reporting on the manuscript:
Robert Armitage, IH Barcelona; Sarah Bailey, Lexis, Malaga; Joanna Bankowska, Lang Ltc, Warsaw; Tim Banks and Shaun Wilden, Akcent, IH Prague; Jodi Bennett, Czech Republic; Klaudia Borecka and Mariusz Mirecki, Lingua Nova, Warsaw; Henny Burke, British Language Centre, Madrid; Nanna Challis, Frances School of English, London; Philip Dale and Samantha Tennant, The Hampstead School of English, London; Rolf Donald, UK; Philippa Louise Dralet, Paris; Andrew Edwins, Greenwich School of English, Warsaw; Liz Kilbey, UK; Jennie Kober, Anglo English School, Hamburg; Adam Kunysz, Poland; John Murphy, Stratford-Upon-Avon; Nicki Pick, Copram, Paris; Christopher Reakirt, The New School of English, Cambridge; Cleide Silva, Brazil; James Tierney, British Council, Milan; Mark Trussell, IH Milan; Anne Vernon-James, IFG Langues, Paris.

We are grateful to the following for permission to reproduce copyright material:
Guardian Newspapers Limited for an adapted extract from 'The Hub' by William Leith, published in *The Observer* 19th July 1998 © The Observer 1998; Independent Newspapers (UK) Limited for an adapted extract from 'The complete guide to the Australian outback' by Steve and Ann Toon, published in *The Independent* 25th September 1999; Little, Brown and Company (UK) for adapted extracts from *Long Walk to Freedom* by Nelson Mandela; The National Magazine Company for an adapted extract from 'Two strangers and a wedding' by Miranda Levy, published in *Cosmopolitan* April 1999; News International Newspapers for adapted extracts from 'Clever Trevor' by Richard Johnson, published in *The Sunday Times* 20th January 2000 © Richard Johnson / Times Newspapers Limited 2000, and 'Urban Scrawl' by Richard Benson, published in *The Sunday Times* 6th August 2000 © Times Newspapers Ltd; and Penguin Books Limited for an adapted extract from *Are You Experienced?* by William Sutcliffe, © William Sutcliffe 1997.

Designed by Steve Pitcher.

Cover design by Juice Creative.

Back cover photographs of the authors by: Trevor Clifford (top) and James Walker (bottom).

Illustrated by: David Atkinson, Philip Bannister, Paul Chambers, Adam Errington (New Division), Flatliner (Debut Art), Rebecca Gibbon (Inkshed), Paul Hampson, Susan Hellard, Matt Herring (Debut Art), Fran Jordan, Peter Lubach, Gill Martin, Ian Mitchell, Louise Morgan (The Art Market), Gavin Reece (New Division), Marco Schaaf, Sue Tewkesbury, Sam Wilson (Inkshed).

Picture research by Hilary Fletcher.

We are grateful to the following for permission to reproduce copyright photographs:
Agency France Presse for 46 (left); Atlantic Syndication for 74; Britstock-IFA / Wirth for 4 (right); Camera Press / Chris Floyd for 47 (left); Charles O'Rear / NGS Image Collection for 72; Corbis / Lindsay Hebberd for 81; Lawrence Manning for 37; Corbis Stock Market / 94 Peter Beek for 26 (bottom left); Carlos Dominguez, CADA Photography for 42 (top); Jon Feingersh for 26 (bottom right); Ariel Skelley for 12 (right); Fortean Picture Library for 105; FPG / Chip Simons for 11; Garden & Wildlife Matters / Martin P Land for 34 (top right); Robert Harding Picture Library / John Miller for 43 (top); Katz Pictures / ©Antonio Pagnotta / Contrasto for 54 (inset); Kingfisher Challenges for 40; 1990, 20th Century Fox (Courtesy Kobal) for 47 (right); The Image Bank / Romilly Lockyer for 5 (top); Eric Meola for 34 (top left); ImageState for 54; First Light for 12 (left); Magnum / Peter Marlow for 31; BARBIE is a trademark owned by and used with the permission of Mattel, Inc. ©2001 Mattel, Inc. All Rights Reserved for 48; News Team / Sean Paget for 30; Oxford Scientific Films / Tony Tifford for 35 (right); PA Photos / EPA for 46 (right); The Photographers Library for 10, 84 (middle), 89 (left), 97; Popperfoto / Reuters for 78; Powerstock Zefa for 20 (bottom); Rex Features for 103; ©Jurgen Schadeberg for 58, 59; South American Pictures / Tony Morrison for 5 (bottom); Frank Spooner Pictures / Gamma for 4 (left); ©Stone / Leland Bobbe for 50; Kaz Chiba for 51; Ken Fisher for 84 (left); Fisher / Thatcher for 84 (right); Bruce Forster for 34 (bottom right); GDT for page 14; Anthony Marsland for 60; Rick Raymond for 36; David Harry Stewart for 9 (top right); Bob Thomas for 106; ©Superstock for 89 (right); Telegraph Colour Library / M.Krasowtiz for 26 (top right) and David Norton for 35 (left).

Front cover photographs left to right: Telegraph Colour Library; Photo Disc; Corbis Stock Market; Superstock; Superstock.

The following photographs were taken on commission for Pearson Education by:
Gareth Boden for 22, 76, 81, 83 and Trevor Clifford for 9 (top left, middle left, bottom right, bottom left), 16, 18, 20 (except bottom), 21, 42 (bottom), 43 (bottom), 48, 49, 56, 75.

Special thanks to the following for their assistance with photographic shoots:
The Galleria Shopping Centre, Hatfield; Laing Homes.